Yorkshire Stories of the Supernatural

Andy Owens

COUNTRYSIDE BOOKS
NEWBURY, BERKSHIRE

First published 1999
© Andy Owens 1999
Reprinted 2002, 2006

COUNTRYSIDE BOOKS
3 Catherine Road
Newbury, Berkshire

ISBN 1 85306 594 3

Designed by Graham Whiteman
Cover painting by Colin Doggett

Produced through MRM Associates Ltd., Reading
Printed by Woolnough Bookbinding Ltd., Irthlingborough

Contents

Acknowledgements

Many thanks to all the people mentioned in this volume and to Jo Outhart, of Treasurer's House; PC Neil Shipman, of Greasbrough; Steve Cliffe, author, psychical researcher and editor of *Stockport Heritage* magazine; Tom Perrott, long-standing member of the Society for Psychical Research and chairman of the Ghost Club; and particularly Chris Ellis.

For Mom, David and Silvie
and especially Dad,
Jack Owens (1924–1998)
who didn't believe in this 'ghost stuff'
– until he saw one!

Foreword

IT has been said that one in ten of us will see a ghost in our lifetime. Could that one-in-ten be you? As England's largest county, the chance of seeing a ghost in Yorkshire is perhaps more likely than being spooked anywhere else. The county of broad acres seems to be crammed with apparitions.

However, do not expect this volume to be a study of myths, legends, traditions and folk tales. This book is a collection of modern encounters with the paranormal, including some first-hand accounts.

From the ghostly grey aeroplanes of the South Yorkshire moors to the multitude of ghosts at Temple Newsam, you will be amazed at the variety of this region's 'other' population. Phantom pilots and ghostly soldiers wander restlessly at RAF Linton-on-Ouse and the site of the Battle of Marston Moor, and a Sheffield couple can never seem to find a house which is *not* haunted. The White Lady of the Whins, the Second-Hand Spook, the Holy Fathers of Bolton Abbey, and the terrifying experiences of Ouija-board users in Whitby, all play their part on this spine-chilling tour of haunted Yorkshire.

And there are others – many others.

If you have your own true ghost story to relate – indeed, if you have encountered an apparition featured in this book – I would be grateful to receive details, c/o my publishers, and perhaps feature it in a future volume.

Whatever ghosts turn out to be – the spirits of our ancestors, or merely recordings of past lives and events – the subject is one which will eventually, no doubt, lead us to a greater understanding of ourselves, and our overall place in the nature of things. That most learned man, Dr Samuel Johnson, considered it to be: 'One of the most important that can come before human understanding. A subject which, after five thousand years, is yet undecided.'

In the meantime – good Ghost-Hunting!

Andy Owens

Not What the Doctor Ordered

WITH no more than a fleeting glance at the grim Victorian façade of Sheffield's Middlewood Hospital, you could be forgiven for wondering what terrors may lurk inside. With its dank red-bricked appearance and foreboding clock tower, the mind could quite easily conjure up images of shadowy figures prowling its creepy corridors and spooky stairwells.

Nestled in a sleepy suburb of Wadsley, over a mile from the bustling centre of neighbouring Hillsborough, time seems to have stood still for this listed building which, along with its multitude of annexes, is now largely disused.

Middlewood was originally opened on 27th August 1872, as the South Yorkshire Asylum, when facilities for the first ever public asylum in Wakefield were judged inadequate and some of the patients subsequently transferred to this institution. In its time it has housed a TB sanatorium, an isolation hospital for intestinal infections, a war hospital between 1915 and 1920, and the Wharncliffe Emergency Hospital which dealt with medical, surgical and neurosis casualties (especially after D-Day and Dunkirk during the Second World War), though it is best remembered locally as a psychiatric hospital.

In the last 20 years it has also gained a notorious reputation as one of the city's most haunted properties. Former staff and patients have come forward to recount various odd events – some of which are still being experienced to this day.

Nurse Jean Higham will never forget what she saw one evening while on night duty in the then notorious Ward 8. Sitting at her desk, she caught sight of a movement out of the corner of her eye, and clearly saw an elderly female patient climb out of bed and set off walking, at a brisk pace, in the opposite direction. Jean was about to call out, but didn't want to wake the other patients, so she stood up and set off after her. Thinking that the old lady was confused and wandering, Jean quickened her pace to reach her, but the patient suddenly turned a sharp right and walked straight through the wall!

As soon as the relief nurse came on duty, Jean excitedly explained what she had seen. To Jean's utter surprise, and her great relief, her colleague rolled her eyes and nodded as if to say 'Oh no, not again.'

For others had seen the elderly patient, Jean being merely the latest in a long line of spooked night staff. Asked to describe her experience to the Ward Sister the following day, she also recalled that the patient had been wearing an old, frilly garment rather than the standard night-dress issued to patients on admittance. The Matron told Jean not to be frightened of the experience, as the elderly lady never did any harm. She was such a regular visitor she was really regarded by the staff as a lucky charm rather than a bad omen.

There are also many accounts concerning the fire-escape door near Ward 11, which seemed to have a mind of its own, bursting open of its own accord. And there was the well-attested account of an elderly man who died on the mixed Hillside Ward, and whose body was kept in a locker overnight, where it proceeded to scare everyone by banging on the door – from the inside!

One of the areas of Middlewood which seems to be the most psychically affected is the staircase by the entrance to Ward 12. The uncanny sound of footsteps hurrying up and down the stairs is frequently reported by members of staff. One such account comes from a former porter whose experiences occurred not during a dark, stormy night as one would expect for a ghost story, but on one of the brightest, sunniest days of summer in 1977.

Henry Gaines, of Derbyshire, was standing at the entrance to Ward 12 and chatting to one of the auxiliaries, when they both clearly heard the distinct sound of footsteps ascending the staircase from the floor below. The sound continued for a few seconds, and they were more than a little surprised when no one appeared.

And then a strange thing happened. The footsteps seemed to transfer themselves from the lower staircase to the corresponding flight of steps which lead up to Ward 13 on the floor above.

Mr Gaines is adamant that no one could have climbed the first staircase, then begun to climb the second, without either he or his colleague having seen them. However, on the off chance that they had been wrong, he set off upstairs to inform the unknown person that Ward 13 was empty and currently out of use. And yet on reaching the doors at the top, the footsteps ceased abruptly and there was no sign of anyone.

There has been a spate of reports in recent years chronicling the curious happenings at Middlewood, and various theories proposed to account for them. One story tells of how a group of student nurses played Ouija in a small room off one of the wards, and failed to smash the glass they were using after the session ended. This has apparently been the undoing of many a haunted householder.

Local writer Valerie Salim, who wrote two books on the history of Sheffield's 'other' population, viewed it as almost inevitable that a building which had housed a psychiatric hospital in its time, may have inherited a permanent reminder of the suffering of those poor souls who were, in many ways, beyond treatment. Says Ms Salim: '. . . it is not surprising that the highly charged emotional atmosphere which can surround mentally disturbed patients should retain the images of past events.'

When the hospital was renovated, the ward numbers were changed round, so that no one particular ward would gain outright notoriety for the disturbances. At that time, a Minister of Religion was asked to exorcise all the spirits as the staff had had enough of mysteries, and it seemed to work for a while, until various phenomena were reported to have returned.

Ghostly goings-on are still reported there from time to time, but then what's all the fuss about? There is no mystery to be solved. There is a perfectly logical and down-to-earth explanation for it all. Middlewood Hospital is haunted!

Haunted Highway

WHEN Transport Minister Paul Channon opened the controversial Stocksbridge bypass on Friday, 13th May 1988, no one could have foreseen the grim death toll which was to follow.

South Yorkshire Police have pointed out that the number of deaths and near pile-ups recorded on the bypass make it no more dangerous than any other road in the area, and that most accidents are down to driver error. However, Stocksbridge town councillors believed that the design of the seven-mile highway, which links the M1 motorway with the A616 Manchester road, was doomed from the beginning and have lobbied for change ever since – with some success. Some parts of the bypass were badly lit, with drivers suddenly plunged into darkness. Motorists coming off the motorway also found the four-lane system suddenly switching to two lanes, and two lanes to one, which made it hazardous for those drivers attempting to overtake.

However, not all of the accidents were down to driver error and poor design of the road. Some motorists claimed to have swerved and crashed due to a mystery figure which glided across the road in front of their cars, and many people have publicly testified to the authenticity of the sightings.

The ghost story itself began quite some time before the official opening of the bypass, when the highway was still under construction. On 7th September 1987, two security guards, David Goldthorpe and Steven Brookes, were patrolling Pearoyd Lane – one of the ancient moorland roads which was being disrupted by the building work. At the time, a new bridge was under construction, to allow the lane to pass over the new bypass, but at this early stage in the work the bridge had not been connected to either side of the lane, so the new structure stood isolated at the side of the old road.

As the two men drove towards the bridge they clearly saw a group of five or six small figures, which they took to be children, dancing in and out of the struts of the bridge. They stopped the car and climbed out, to warn them that it was dangerous to play there, but the children had vanished and they found no footprints in the undisturbed mud at that point.

Puzzled, they returned to their car and set off further down Pearoyd Lane, until they glimpsed an odd figure on the parapet at the side of the bridge. Mr Goldthorpe shone the car headlights at the figure, which looked like a monk wearing a habit, but their beam disappeared. The two men were now so scared that they roused a local vicar from his sleep, and begged him to carry out an exorcism at the spot. Their employer, Mr Michael Lee, saw them later, and testified that they were both panic-stricken at the encounter, needing considerable sick leave to recover from the experience.

Deepcar police station greeted the reported incident with much scepticism, but they had not heard the last of it. Just five days later, on the evening of Saturday 12th September, two police officers had an experience which was even stranger.

Police Constable Dick Ellis was on car patrol at the bypass, accompanied by Special Constable John Beet, when they decided they would take a short run up to Pearoyd Lane, without radioing through to base. It was a clear moonlit night when the two constables parked up at the side of the lane, facing the bridge. On the bridge stood a white-painted pallet box, and as the pair looked on, they noticed an odd black shadow flitting across it, which darted round the back, then round to the front again. Intrigued by this, they climbed out of the car and approached the box, only to find that the shadow had vanished. Having dismissed it as an illusion, they returned to their car and – wouldn't you know it – the shadow had returned!

While they were discussing this puzzling sight, PC Ellis experienced what he later described as 'a horrible chill' which coursed right through him. From his position in the driving seat, with the window wound down, he had the odd and rather unnerving feeling that someone was standing behind him at the side of the car. He quickly turned to see a figure in light-coloured clothing with a 'V' shape on its chest, who then vanished and re-appeared at the passenger door. When Constable Beet saw the figure he cried out in alarm. According to him, it was dressed very differently – a man in 'Dickensian' clothing who just stared in at the officer. As Beet stared back, he found it hard to focus on the figure, until it vanished.

When the two men had sufficiently composed themselves, Ellis tried to contact Deepcar police station on the car radio, but as he did so, they both felt several heavy thumps on the back of the car. They didn't stick around long enough to discover who or what had caused them!

Later, when being interviewed for the Michael Aspel TV programme *Strange . . . But True?*, PC Ellis said he would normally have dismissed it as his imagination, if his partner had not seen it too, and felt the same eerie sensation. He said it was very unnerving and that the whole thing was not fabricated, adding that the police don't do 'that sort of thing'.

The programme also screened a reconstruction of the sightings of the ghostly children, with the help of pupils from local Wharncliffe Side primary school. There have been many witnesses of this curious sight, including Ms Barbara Lee, of the Midhopestones Arms, who saw them playing in a field in March 1995. She described the sighting as weird, both because of their appearance and that they were playing in a field above the new bridge, miles away from where children usually play. The children were happily dancing in a circle together, with the girls dressed in pinafores and mob caps, and the boys in breeches, which reminded her of late 17th/early 18th-century clothing.

Child-minder Ms Pat Heathcote corroborated the story, having witnessed a similar sight just three weeks previously. She watched about eight children in long black skirts and white pinafores dancing around what seemed like an invisible maypole, on a grass mound near the new bridge.

As far as I know, the odd events witnessed by the security guards have not been reported by anyone else, and although the children are seen from time to time, the majority of eyewitness testimonies have concerned a monk.

Sightings of this particular apparition have been so common, and reported by the *Sheffield Star* so regularly, that a local lady, Ms Katrina Hewitt, was moved to recall stories of the phantom monk she was told of by her grandmother who lived in a cottage at White Row Farm, Hunshelf, many years ago. According to the story that she was told as a child, the phantom is that of a monk who was killed by soldiers on the surrounding moors, and is still wandering the vicinity to this day.

The sightings of the monk have continued over the last few years. In 1990, lorry driver Melbourne Heptinstall had an odd experience. He had just pulled off the road into Deepcar and came to a halt in the trailer park on Station Road. While he busied himself with the job of untying the ropes fastened to his trailer, a cold chill came over him and he noticed a strange, musty-like smell. Looking up, he watched what he described as 'a monk-like figure' gliding through his headlights.

Other odd incidents have been reported which may or may not have anything to do with the haunting. In 1992, Elizabeth Howard and her boyfriend, from Chapeltown, were driving along the bypass when the car was suddenly engulfed in a very strong smell of pipe tobacco. The windows were closed, and neither was smoking at the time (and never smoked a pipe anyway) so how the smell originated greatly puzzles them to this day.

In December 1994, following the media coverage that the bypass hauntings had gained from the *Strange . . . But True?* programme, Stocksbridge became what the local newspapers termed 'a mecca for ghost-hunters', as more and more tourists flocked to the area. The then town mayor, Councillor Betty Dickinson, publicly welcomed the nationwide interest as it was boosting the local economy. She did not believe in the ghosts herself, even though her own son, Tim Dickinson, had seen the monk. Interested parties were holding regular vigils at the Pearoyd Lane site with cameras at the ready, hoping to capture evidence of the ghosts on film. Although no such evidence was forthcoming, the sightings from local people continued unabated.

One person had been collating information on the sightings of the monk and also the mysterious 'black presence' which some people have sensed and associated with the ghost. Psychic consultant Lucinda Jane Beevers of Penistone, near Barnsley, said she had encountered the apparition herself while driving home via the bypass. While she was used to dealing with spirits in her work, she had never felt such a sudden and unnerving sense of fear as when a dark shape appeared in her car next to her. The 'presence' she sensed and saw was very large in size and very frightening. She quickly recited the Lord's Prayer and the figure promptly vanished. Eight of her clients had had identical experiences and she is convinced that it is a very real haunting. On another occasion, Ms Beevers saw the shadowy figures appear in somebody else's car which was travelling ahead of her. When she overtook the car, the big, black shape vanished. While most of the sightings have been centred around Pearoyd Lane and the adjacent bridge, she found that people had encountered the frightening presence – and the figure of the monk – over a wider area; a three-mile stretch of the bypass between Stocksbridge and Wortley, near Sheffield. Ms Beevers explained that although the monk instils fear into the hearts of people it is not an evil spirit – just very troubled, and it may need the help of several mediums working together to move it on.

Her research had uncovered an old legend which seemed to throw light on how the haunting originated. Tying in with Katrina Hewitt's account, it concerned a monk who lived at Hunshelf Hall. His last wish to be buried at nearby Stannington was ignored and he was subsequently laid to rest in unhallowed ground. She pointed out that the ghost of the monk had been haunting the area for many years, but seemed to have been disturbed when the construction of the bypass began.

There are very few incidents where ghosts have deliberately caused physical harm to people, but psychological damage can be suffered and Ms Beevers believed that the monk may have been the inadvertent cause of some of the car crashes on the ill-fated bypass. She obtained testimonies from 15 drivers who had reported picking out the figure in their headlights and seeing or sensing the presence in their cars.

One of the more recent sightings of the monk occurred on New Year's Eve, 1997, when deputy supermarket manager Paul Ford, and his wife Jane, an advertising manager, had a near-fatal crash while driving along the bypass on their way to visit Mrs Ford's sister.

Mr Ford spotted the figure as they approached the part of the road which borders a steep embankment overlooking the British Steelworks Corporation premises at Stocksbridge. He said that from a distance it just looked like someone trying to cross the road, but when they got nearer, they could clearly see it was a man in a long cloak. When Mr Ford realised that the figure had no face, and was actually hovering several feet above the road, he froze with fear and suddenly let go of the steering wheel.

Acting quickly, his wife grabbed the wheel as the car swerved, and he slammed the brakes on, bringing the vehicle to a halt. Mr Ford said that if it wasn't for his wife's quick thinking, or if she hadn't been there, he probably would have been killed that night. When the couple finally reached their destination, Paul Ford was white with fear and shaking uncontrollably. They told the *Sheffield Star* that it had been a very frightening experience and could explain why there had been so many fatal accidents on the road. They both pledged never to return to the bypass and warned that the ghost could be a grave hazard to more drivers if something was not done about it.

After that incident there followed many similar sightings from drivers, some of whom have had to seek counselling following their encounters. But something was to be done about it.

In the programme *For the love of . . . Ghosts*, screened in 1998, presenter Jon Ronson gathered together six ghost investigators to discuss the subject and one of them, a medium, claimed to have helped the spirit of the monk pass on to the spirit world. Sheffield bus inspector Dave Williamson, who helped to form a 'ghostbusting' group of psychics from Sheffield's 'Mainline' bus company, claimed to have contacted the spirit of the monk with the assistance of his colleagues. Having spoken to the monk, Dave learned that the monk thought they were 'witches' coming to hurt him. As soon as Dave talked of God, the monk calmed, and he was thus able to help him pass on to the next stage of being.

The monk of Stocksbridge Bypass has not been seen since – but as for the ghostly children, perhaps it is only a matter of time?

Phantom Flyers at Linton-on-Ouse

RAF LINTON-ON-OUSE was opened on 13th May 1937 and formed part of No 4 Bomber Command. Although the headquarters were initially located at Mildenhall, in Suffolk, they were transferred to Linton just one month later. The Command was headed by Air Commodore A.T. Harris, or 'Bomber' Harris as he was later to be known.

Aircraft from the base participated in many of the night-time bombing raids on Germany and Norway, and it was host to many different squadrons, including those of the Canadian Air Force. As on all Bomber Command stations, death was frequent and losses high during the years of the Second World War. Since 1957, Linton has been the No 1 Flying Training School, training over 50 new recruits there every year, from both the Royal Air Force and the Royal Navy.

With the many deaths of pilots and ground personnel alike over the years, it is perhaps no wonder that the airfield has become the haunt of not one, but several spirits.

The ghostly goings-on first hit the headlines in July 1988, when assistant air traffic controller Brenda Jenkinson saw a shadowy figure one night in the control tower. As she was later to recount at a press conference organised by the base public relations officer, Squadron Leader Michael Brooks, Brenda and her colleagues were on night flying duties in the control room. She had just come out of the switchboard room, on her way to the met. office when she saw a tall, broad-shouldered figure in a flying jacket. Frozen with fear, she stared hard at the man, recalling afterwards that she could see right through him. He moved slowly towards the approach room and then disappeared.

Brenda was petrified. She looked around her and, finding there was no-one else there screamed, 'I've just seen a ghost!' When an officer rushed to find out what all the noise was about, she hurriedly told him of what had happened. Together, they searched the immediate area, but found no trace of the man.

For the next three nights, Brenda positioned herself at exactly the same spot, at exactly 10 pm, hoping to catch another glimpse of the figure – without success. Two months had passed before she saw it again. She had almost forgotten the incident when, one night, Brenda was coming down from the glass tower at the top of the building, with Flight Lieutenant Mark Byrne behind her. She happened to glance into the tea room, just off the first floor landing and saw the same, shadowy figure standing by the door.

'Did you see that?' she asked her colleague. 'Yes,' he nodded.

When Brenda and Mark became a laughing stock at the base, Squadron Leader Michael Brooks went out on a limb to stand by them by taking the unusual step of issuing a full press statement about the ghost. He also arranged to hold a press conference for the local papers but, perhaps inevitably, the national press got hold of it and journalists from the *Daily Express, Daily Mirror* and the *Sun* descended on the base, as well as various TV camera crews.

Michael Brooks was certainly taking the matter seriously. He had found two other members of staff who claimed to have seen the figure, and he had also arranged to fly Brenda back from her new post at Anglesey for the day, so she could attend the conference. He stated publicly that the ghost was much more than just a curiosity: it could prove to have disastrous results by appearing in the control tower, as this could distract the traffic controllers from their duties, which required great concentration. Having said that, he did state that there was no question of exorcism at that point, because the presence did not seem in any way consciously malignant to anyone working there.

After the conference and subsequent media coverage, Brenda flew back to Anglesey and that, for the time being, was that.

In November 1988, BBC producer Martin O'Collins had been commissioned to make a documentary for BBC2 called *Ghost Train*, concerning accounts of the paranormal. In his research, he had met a medium called Eddie Burks who devoted much time to releasing spirits from their earthly confines – or 'ghostbusting' as the media like to call it – and therefore asked Eddie if he would mind visiting a haunted site and being filmed making contact with a spirit. When the medium agreed, Martin O'Collins chose RAF Linton-on-Ouse as a perfect setting for the documentary, but was careful not to disclose any information regarding the location, or details of the haunting, to Eddie beforehand.

That same month, Eddie Burks arrived at the base, accompanied by Martin with his camera, microphones, lights and recording equipment. There they met up with Squadron Leader Brooks and Ms Jenkinson, who had laid on a buffet to welcome the medium to Linton.

Martin was particularly interested in the theory that the ghost was that of Flight Engineer Walter Frederick Hodgson, whose details had been given out at the press conference a few months ago, though Eddie Burks did point out that the spirit could turn out to be someone quite different.

The story of Hodgson's life was certainly an illustrious one and Mr O'Collins knew it would make an excellent story on screen. Stationed at Linton during the Second World War, Hodgson left the base for a bombing raid on Essen, in Germany. He was one of the crew in the twelve Halifax bombers of 78 Squadron chosen for the raid. Following the mission, only three of the planes returned to the base, with Hodgson's having been shot down that night.

Luckily, Hodgson bailed out, landing safely in Holland, where he was given shelter by a brave Dutch family. However, the very next day, their little daughter excitedly told her classmates about the Englishman, and the Germans quickly got word. He was then arrested and marched off by soldiers to the prisoner of war camp Stalag Luft 3.

21

Walter was one of the few prisoners who broke out of Stalag Luft 3 and 4, which was later immortalised in the movie *The Great Escape*, with Steve McQueen. His sister, Mrs Olive Johnson said that her brother was only free for a couple of hours after the break-out. Frightened and injured, when caught by six German soldiers, 'he told me he would forever remember a fat German woman spitting in his face, as one of the soldiers pointed a revolver at him.' When the film was premiered in London his family had accompanied Walter to the first showing.

A silver plaque, donated to the base by Hodgson's family in 1959, was attached to the outside of the control tower at Linton. It reads: 'W.F. Hodgson, born 19th Feb 1921, in Hull, and held as a prisoner at Stalag 3 and 4. He died of tuberculosis, in 1959, at the age of 38'. Michael Brooks said that at the time of Brenda's first encounter, the plaque had been moved to the inside of the control tower. He suggested that Walter Hodgson's spirit began haunting because of its relocation, which may have upset him.

Hodgson's surviving relatives were more than a little alarmed on reading that Walter's spirit might have returned. His sister Mrs Johnson, although sceptical declared she was prepared to 'stand on the runway at midnight in pitch black if necessary', saying that her brother was a gentle man, not a haunting person. His widow, Mrs Audrey Hodgson, however, believed her husband could well be the ghost, because she recalled that his last, dearest wish had been carried out – that his ashes be scattered across the runway at Linton. And she passed on a welcome message to Brenda not to be afraid. She said he would never harm anyone – it was just that he loved Linton so much; the RAF and the base were the cornerstones of his life.

However, whether Hodgson's spirit was indeed among those who had returned to the base, one thing was shortly made quite clear by Eddie Burks. The ghost of the control tower was not Hodgson.

The medium made his way to the first floor landing by the tea room, accompanied by Michael, Martin and Brenda, where the latter had seen the figure on the second occasion. Mr Burks paced around the landing for a few seconds, until he announced that he had someone (a spirit) with him and that, due to a sudden pain in his back, he needed to sit down on the stairs for a while.

He explained the impression that was apparently being channelled to him from the spirit. He thought this man had been killed on the airfield, in the late 1950s or early 1960s. It was an ordinary accident; knocked down by a vehicle at night. The man's back was broken and he was in a lot of pain (Eddie, like many mediums, explained that a trapped spirit often impressed the experience of death, and any injuries sustained, on the channeller, which is why he needed to rest on the stairs). The man had been put on a stretcher and carried into the control tower, but died soon after. There was a great weight on the dead man's mind. He felt he had not prepared himself or his family for his sudden demise, and didn't seem to understand that a lot of time had passed since his accident. That is why he kept appearing in the control tower – with much unfinished business.

Eddie then turned to Brenda and Michael. He said, someone is thanking Brenda for her help in bringing this to the attention of others; for her courage in coming back and waiting to make contact. Eddie then related how a feeling of light and lightness was coming through to him. He said that a team of spirit helpers had come forward to take the man into their care. 'God Bless,' they said to Mr Burks. 'Leave him to us.' After a moment, Eddie added: 'He's free now.'

After the experience, Brenda was choking back tears, particularly when the spirit thanked her for helping him. Michael Brooks, too, was speechless.

Martin had filmed the spectacle and, while he was pleased at having done so for his documentary, he wondered if there would be enough material. It was suggested that the team should take lunch, then see if there were any more spirits lingering at the base!

Some time after Brenda's experience, a cleaner at the base for 14 years, Mrs Betty Fenwick, had reported having seen a figure in the Officers' Mess building nearby, so the team made their way to the first floor bedroom where the sighting took place. The shadowy figure was said to be that of another man in RAF uniform and a Biggles-type flying helmet, sitting in one of the armchairs. On being questioned about it, Mrs Fenwick said it was a very peaceful presence, and added that she could often sense him – and others – at the base. Mrs Fenwick didn't know the man's name and just referred to him as 'Old Fred'.

Eddie sank down into the armchair and immediately sensed the airman. He explained that the man was an extrovert, likeable sort, completely dedicated to his task of flying planes for the base. Therefore, he felt it was very difficult to leave this world and head off towards the spirit world as he should do. Eddie contacted his spirit helpers and led them to him, explaining that they would try and persuade him to leave.

Just before the team left Linton, Michael asked Eddie to walk down a corridor in the Officers' Mess which he thought was haunted. As Eddie walked along the corridor, he said he felt a great sense of joy and excitement and the sudden urge to start running. He was watching the image of a young lady running towards a man who had just appeared at the end of the corridor, and now they were embracing each other. Eddie explained that the couple were married. The man had been sent on a bombing mission and was reported 'lost in action'. However, he turned up alive a few days later, and had now been reunited with his wife.

Eddie added that this probably wasn't a haunting at all; the man and woman were not ghosts in the accepted sense of the word. He explained that it was no more than a psychic echo, imprinted on the environment by the strong emotions being displayed by the pair, and it was perfectly possible that the man and his wife were still alive.

At the end of the visit, Martin O'Collins knew that he had more than enough film for his documentary, but, nonetheless, would have liked to discover the identity of the two ghostly airmen. Michael Brooks went to the York Reference Library to see if he could corroborate the stories with facts reported in the press.

He did. It appeared that the ghost of the control tower could have been one AC1 Thomas Davies, aged 21, who was killed while directing a vehicle on the airfield, on 27th July 1950. The airman in the bedroom at the Officers' Mess building, corresponded to Flight Lieutenant Robert Arthur Hatton Rogers, aged 29, who died due to pilot error on 1st June 1978 as his Jet Provost plane was performing aerobatics over the base, when it caught fire and hit the ground. Although he had ejected just before impact, he still suffered multiple injuries and died shortly afterwards.

I wonder how many more ghosts and spirits wander the scores of other military bases around Britain and the rest of the world, waiting to be released from this life into the next, by people like Eddie Burks?

4

Ghostly Goings-on at the Haunted Club

THERE is a public house on Townsgate in Wyke, Bradford, called 'The Hypnotist', after its landlord Edward Mann – an internationally renowned hypnotist of many years' standing. Perhaps he should have called it the 'The Ghost' since there is at least one spectral visitor here who has frightened cleaners and pub regulars alike. Although the ghost was regularly discussed by the locals no one told the owner about it for some time after he moved in and, although Mr Mann has heard sincere testimonies from alleged witnesses, he remains unconvinced.

One man flatly refuses to go into the toilets on his own! One evening someone tapped him on the shoulder and asked, 'Are you alright, Sam?' When Sam turned round, it was to find there was no one there. He even ran out of the toilets without doing up his trousers! Mr Mann's boxer dog would usually have no trouble tackling unwanted intruders, but one night he ran yelping out of the old darkened dance hall for no apparent reason and he, too, steers well clear of the gents' toilets, and will often make a wide detour round the door. Even the cleaners refuse to enter them alone. They will only work in pairs – because they say that on more than one occasion, the toilets have flushed by themselves.

On Hallowe'en 1985, Mr Mann was reported in the local paper to be issuing a challenge to the ghost – known as 'Fred' – to appear at midnight. He said that if Fred showed up, he and his regulars would make him very welcome. Unfortunately, he didn't.

However, this was not the first time the ghost of the pub had hit the headlines. The inn was originally converted from an old clubhouse, the Wyke non-political club, which stood on the site. Successive relief managers refused to stay on the premises overnight, and former cleaners also have their tales to tell.

On 4th October 1972, a story about the haunting was splashed across the pages of a local newspaper, concerning various experiences at the club. Several of the staff claimed to have seen the ghost, including one Christine Jenkins, a former police-woman and judo instructor, who stayed behind at the club one evening with club secretary John Hall, the relief steward, and a married couple. Before leaving, she went to the ladies' toilets and, on opening the door, came face to face with a stranger. Ms Jenkins describes him as middle-aged with grey hair. His eyes were glassy and staring, and he was wearing a dark suit which appeared to be soaking wet.

When he didn't move out of her way, she grabbed the door handle and pulled with all her might, feeling his 'cold, clammy hand' with four fingers but no thumb, under her own. When she eventually pushed past him, she felt someone tugging at her jumper trying to hold her back, and she fainted. Her four colleagues found her, and when she came round she told them what had happened. Some of them had had similar experiences. Ms Jenkins later found that the original site of the club had once been a millhouse dam and that the ghost was said to be that of an engineer who drowned there many years ago. This would seem to explain the wet clothes. An elderly resident of Wyke said that the man had lost one of his thumbs in an industrial accident.

As usual, media sensationalism stepped in and a curious encounter with a ghost became a story headline: 'Trapped in the loo by the fearsome phantom'. People were quoted as being 'horrified', 'terrified', 'a bag of nerves', and were left 'white and shaking' – yet nothing the alleged ghost did suggested that he was actually threatening in any way.

There were certainly many unnerving incidents. Mrs Mary

Ferguson entered the dressing room situated at the side of the stage in the concert hall, which was often noted for its 'terribly oppressive atmosphere' and was almost invariably cold. Sitting on the steps which lead down to the room from the stage was a figure of a man aged around 40. He was wearing a long raincoat and was leaning forward, resting his head on his hand – and a second later he was gone.

Fellow cleaners had similar experiences. Mrs Mary Robson has often felt a sudden chill which steals across the floor while she is cleaning the concert room, sending a shiver across her neck and back. One morning the cleaners found a table and four chairs which had been lifted onto the stage, with four wet ring marks from glasses on the table, yet the club had been closed the previous night, and the steward said no one had been present when he locked up for the night and left.

Former club committee chairman Harry Tillotson stated that although he remained largely sceptical, there must surely be something to account for the strange phenomena reported, as many of the witnesses were friends of his, and he did not doubt their word. Mr Tillotson volunteered to do much of the maintenance work at the club and, although he spent many days and evenings working there alone, he had no experiences himself. The sightings continued, however, for many years.

Club secretary John Hall used to laugh at the idea of the ghost – until he saw it, too. In September 1972, he was cleaning up after the club had closed together with steward Jimmy Cahill and Mrs Cahill, when the steward thought he heard someone else moving about. Mr Hall went to the games room to investigate and saw, in a darkened corner, a man with light hair and wearing a dark suit. He shouted to the Cahills to switch on the lights, but when they flickered on, the man had gone.

Mr Hall said that previous stewards of the club had had their own odd experiences. One had watched the main light rapidly flicker on and off and yet subsequent checks to the electricity supply and switches drew a blank.

The landlord of The Hypnotist, Mr Mann, has said that while he does not believe in the supernatural, he has witnessed various odd things, for which he would be hard pushed to find a rational explanation. Toilets flush on their own, lights switch on and off, and on one occasion he saw the spotlight over the dartboard seemingly turning round of its own accord!

5

The Howden Triangle

O<small>N</small> 18<small>TH</small> May 1945, just ten days after the Second World War had ended, the six-man crew of Lancaster KB993, part of the Royal Canadian Air Force 'Goose' Squadron, took off from RAF Linton-on-Ouse, for what was to be their final flight. The emblem of a Canadian goose displayed proudly on her side with the badge motto 'For Freedom', the Lancaster left the base for a training exercise – and never returned.

The Canadian 'Goose' squadron had been formed at Lindholme in 1941 – just one of many RCAF squadrons which served at Allied bases overseas. This particular crew consisted of Flying Officer Anthony Arthur Clifford and his experienced men: Bomb Aimer 'Scratch' Fehrman, Wireless Operator 'Blood and Guts' Cameron, Air Gunners 'Hairless Joe' Halvorson and 'Rabbit' Hellerson, and Flight Engineer 'Gassless' McIver. Their first operational flight was to bomb railway marshalling yards in June 1941, and then they flew Hampdens when they were part of the first 1,000 bomber raid against Cologne in May 1942.

With the war over, and no new missions planned, Group HQ at Linton was hard pushed to find activities to keep the men occupied and so crews were often sent out on fighter affiliation, cross-country flights and 'circuits and bumps' training. This latter was a routine on-going exercise for all air crews, to practise landings and take-offs, and it was with this objective that the Lancaster crew took off that day.

The squadron crews were in fact just counting the days to 20th June, when they were due to fly the brand new Canadian-built

Lancaster X bombers back to their original home in Canada. They were to be given a good send-off by the local people and their British colleagues at the base, at a specially-arranged 'open home' day. However, having taken off from Linton, almost exactly a month before their proposed flight home, it seems that the crew must have grown bored with the circuits-and-bumps training exercise and decided to take a circular tour of the region instead.

From their position at Linton, in North Yorkshire, they passed over South Yorkshire, sweeping across the moorlands, towards the Derbyshire border. However, it seems that they got lost in the complete darkness of the moors. Ironically, their navigator, 'Gee Sam', had not accompanied them on their flying exercise; his skills were not thought to be needed by the crew as they had only been cleared for local flying. Luckily, they spotted the lights of the town of Glossop, which must have been a great relief for them. As the war had ended, with no further fear of an air attack, the blackout restrictions had been lifted, and the crew circled the town for a short time while they got their bearings.

No doubt deciding to fly back to Linton, they pulled out of the circular run and, watched by local boy Ken Bancroft standing on the steps of his father's workshop, they straightened up, heading off for the east. Mr Bancroft was still watching as the Lancaster approached the Peaks, some of which rise to 2,000 feet. It was passing over them and rapidly nearing the South Yorkshire moors when it hit one of them at full speed, and burst into a ball of flame. Mr Bancroft sprinted to the local police station and, finally convinced that he wasn't making it all up, they sent someone to investigate. Five of the crew died instantly; the rear gunner survived for a while having been pulled clear of the wreckage by a rescuer, but nothing could be done to save him.

On 20th June 1945, the crews of 408 Goose Squadron left Linton for Canada, leaving behind one of its Lancasters impaled on a moorland peak, and six of its men, who had braved the war over Germany only to be tragically killed in routine training.

However this, it seems, was not the end of the matter, for that date seemed to mark the beginning of a worrying trend. Just two months later – and 50 yards away from the same site – a USAF Dakota crashed in similar circumstances killing its seven-man crew. And the tragic history has continued to this day, with over 50 planes, in as many years, coming down over the moors.

Former airman, Ron Collier, who has extensively researched the subject and written two books plotting the sites of the crashes, has proposed a possible scientific explanation for the crashes. He suggests that there is a prevailing south-westerly wind which blows the planes off their flightpaths to Manchester and Liverpool.

However, it is not only the mystery of multiple crashes that perplexes local people. What of the 'ghostly grey aeroplanes' which have been spotted flying low over houses in the area, which then seem to plunge down into the peaty bogs of the moorland – and disappear without trace?

Mr Collier says that there must be a logical explanation for the numerous crashes, though he has repeatedly come up against the paranormal during his research. He has met many people who say they have been contacted by dead airmen. One lady had been using a Ouija board with a group of friends, when they received the message: 'Where we are now, we are not at rest', and then it proceeded to list all the names of the crew members of another tragedy which befell a Superfortress plane in 1948. He has also heard from a farmer who retrieved bits of the wreckage which remain at some of the crash sites, taking them back to his farm to use as spare parts for farming equipment. He said that he and his son watched the outhouse where he stored them suddenly begin to shake uncontrollably. The two decided to return the wreckage to the original site. Vague figures of the poor souls who perished have also been glimpsed by hikers, campers and motorists, who are now wary of returning to the moors at night.

Indeed, the 40 square miles covering Howden Moor, Bolsterstone Moor and the misty peat bogs of the Peak District have become known as The Howden Triangle. This area has proved to be a graveyard for many of the 300 military airmen and civilian pilots who have lost their lives there, as numerous searches have been called off, with rescue teams unable or unwilling to venture further into this forbidding and inhospitable moorland.

Tales of ghostly planes and phantom pilots have become interwoven into the rich traditional folklore of the area and would merely be remembered as colourful, if not fanciful, myths – had the crashes and sightings been a thing of the past. However, planes continue to crash here to this day, and accounts of spine-chilling encounters are still being reported to local newspapers.

The most recent crash was in 1990, when private pilot Walter Cubitt, of Norwich, came down on nearby Broomhead Moor, while on his way to an air show in Blackpool. The moors were not en route to Blackpool, the flying conditions were not hazardous, and his flying club couldn't imagine what he was doing flying over this area. Mr Cubitt was a very experienced pilot – so why his plane came down on the moorland will remain a mystery. Again, rescue teams considered it too hazardous and, ultimately, pointless, to continue their search, hence his body was never recovered and remains entombed in the quagmires to this day.

And, as fast as planes go down, so the inexplicable sightings of 'ghost planes' increase.

In April 1994, retired postman Tony Ingle was walking his dog near the hill which overlooks the crash sites of the Lancaster and Dakota. Only a week after a plaque was unveiled at that spot to commemorate the airmen who lost their lives in the area, Tony, and his dog Ben, had an experience that would haunt them forever. Suddenly, the sunshine overhead was blocked out by a propeller-driven plane, which Tony later identified as a Dakota, which flew very low towards the hill, and disappeared over it.

Tony described the sighting as bizarre. He said he could see the propellers going round yet there was no sound at all – just a deathly silence. He could see the plane banking, as if trying to turn, when it disappeared over a hedge on the crest of the hill. He and Ben sprinted to the top, convinced that it had come down, only to find an empty field. He said there was no sign of the plane.

Since that day, Tony has returned to that field, but Ben refuses to go anywhere near it. The only time Tony tried to force him, the dog snapped his collar and ran off. He added that he was not one to believe in ghosts and always laughed at the suggestion of supernatural apparitions, but now he is unsure. He saw that plane as clear as day – and it disappeared before his eyes.

Almost two years later, on 25th March 1997, a similar incident sparked a huge moorland search, and national TV news coverage.

On the evening of Monday the 24th, dozens of worried people jammed phone lines to South Yorkshire Police, saying that a large aircraft displaying navigation lights had flown very low over their homes and was clearly in trouble. Even though the Civil Aviation Authority had no reports of missing aircraft, police treated the callers seriously, as they were very specific in description and many of them tallied in detail. They quickly instigated a round-the-clock search involving police with tracker dogs, fire crews, three helicopters, mountain rescue teams and over 100 civilian volunteers.

Among the callers were former special police constable Mariafrance Tattersfield and her husband Steven of Wharncliffe Side, near Sheffield, who were out driving on Bolsterstone Moor, hoping to catch a glimpse of the Hale-Bopp comet which could be seen at that time of year. At 10.15 pm, they saw a prop-driven plane which was flying very, very low, descending towards the ground at a rapid speed, looking as if it was heading for a crash-landing. There were lights on the wings and it was descending at less than 1,000 feet. Unlike Tony Ingle's encounter, the sight was accompanied by the low droning sound which you would get with a Second World War bomber. Mr Tattersfield is a former pilot and so was under no illusion about what they were both looking at. They watched, astonished, as it seemed to plunge down behind trees to the peat bogs around Broomhead reservoir.

Another group of people in the area, who were looking for the comet through a telescope, said they watched an object trailing smoke, followed by a strange red glow on the moors.

Gamekeeper Michael Ellison, and his wife, Barbara, rushed outside their home in Strines, near the Strines Inn, after hearing an almighty explosion, which literally shook the house. Mr Ellison subsequently searched the immediate area of the moors without success, but a police officer investigating their call saw what he thought was a plume of smoke rising from the moors towards the Woodhead area. Rescue teams also heard from a farmer who had instinctively ducked when a plane passed directly overhead, while other witnesses saw a long, dark object, with lights on its wings and tail, descending rapidly into Bolsterstone.

In fact, a full investigation revealed that over 60 people from Dronfield, near Sheffield, to Barnsley had reported seeing what was believed to be the same plane, at the same time, on the same night. Not only had people witnessed the plane, and seen smoke rising from the supposed crash site, but experts at Edinburgh University revealed they had recorded a sonic boom from that area on their sensitive equipment at exactly the same time – which suggested that something had indeed crashed to earth.

The search lasted an exhausting 18 hours, until it was finally called off the next day. South Yorkshire fire and rescue crews from Sheffield and Barnsley, and the West Yorkshire police helicopter, had all been drafted in to assist with the search – and all returned to base tired and confused.

Various claims had been made on that fateful night which were still under investigation. Detectives from Sheffield examined footage of a plane taken by two teenagers that evening, which was never identified. The RAF and MOD denied there was any military activity in the area after two groups of people reported a large, black triangular object being chased by what looked like two Tornado fighter jets. They also denied claims by Leeds-based *UFO Magazine* that a top-secret RPV (remotely piloted vehicle) used on spying missions, had crashed on the moors and been recovered in an undercover operation.

However, none of this seemed to have any relevance to the sighting of Second World War planes that night. Due to the number of witnesses who all made identical reports, a hoax would have to be ruled out. For the same reason, hallucinations, illusions and atmospheric phenomena could not be applicable in this case. So what is the answer?

Ron Collier pointed out that virtually each crash site has its own legend, and for as long as he could remember people have been seeing mystery aircraft plunging down on the moors and there have been fruitless searches for them. Often people report seeing things like stars or balloons but this most recent sighting was different due to the number of witnesses involved, each corroborating the other's story – and an explosion was heard as well. If it was a real aircraft then someone would have identified it by now.

This no-nonsense former airman adds that there is a force which governs these moors. You can feel it. And the scores of sightings only back that up. Many of them are from plain-speaking farmers who know better than to believe in ghost stories. Something is going on – and it is very hard to explain what.

It's a mystery – and it's just one of those mysteries that will probably never be solved.

6

Old Soldiers Die Hard

ONE of the bloodiest skirmishes of the Civil War began on the afternoon of 2nd July 1644 at Marston Moor, in North Yorkshire. The artillery duel was to last a full two hours, with continuous fighting raging between the Royalist army led by Prince Rupert and Cromwell's Parliamentarians.

Cromwell's brave soldiers stood their ground despite each fierce Royalist attack, and Cromwell himself was slashed in the neck by a Cavalier colonel named Marcus Trevor. Prince Rupert's men were cut down with each onslaught, until the dead and dying lay scattered across the battlefield. With each advance, the Roundheads' muskets continued to thin the ranks of their attackers, until few remained.

When a section of the Royalist forces broke the formation and fled, Cromwell ordered his men to chase them across the moor and pick them off in their retreat. When that was accomplished, they turned back to face the infantry led by the Marquis of Newcastle, and eventually defeated them too. With Cromwell victorious, the Royalist cause had been dealt a powerful and deadly blow. Over 4,000 Cavaliers died on that summer evening in the county of York. A memorial was eventually placed at the site to commemorate those who died at the Battle of Marston Moor and there it remains to this day.

It is not difficult to imagine almost anything supernatural appearing in this isolated spot, just under a mile from the village of Long Marston, which has seen such a violent and bloody history. And, while there are various legends connected to the site, which have been woven into the folklore of the place, there are several recorded accounts of people who have happened across ghostly soldiers of yesteryear. The country road which winds through Marston Moor today forms part of the A59 which often remains unmarked on road maps. It is the only accessible route to the moors for motorists, and it is from here that people have experienced the phenomena.

The first recorded sighting was in November 1932, when commercial traveller Tom Horner and his friend Arthur Wright, were travelling in Horner's car from York to Harrogate. As they passed Marston Moor station, Horner pulled over slightly to let a bus pass which was travelling in the opposite direction. Wright suddenly shouted for his friend to stop. Horner had not seen the trio of men who had just appeared in front of the car. As Horner slammed on the brakes, he and his companion watched the men as they walked ahead of them, never more than 20 yards away at any one time.

Their appearance was curious to say the least. They were all dressed in long cloaks, wide-brimmed hats with cockades, long-top boots, and each had shoulder-length hair. For the life of them, the two observers could not understand why the men were dressed as Cavaliers. The three men appeared so solid and life-like, that Horner and Wright did not consider for a moment that they were looking at ghosts.

They watched them for a good ten minutes, as the weary and haggard looking trio turned to the right across the moors, and then, in an instant, they were gone. As the car continued on its course, the two men scoured the moorlands searching for any glimpse of the curiously attired group, but they were nowhere to be seen.

When they were questioned later by a newspaper reporter, Arthur Wright – who had seen them first – said that the bus driver did not react to the men as he and his friend had done, and it could be that neither the driver nor passengers saw them. Wright said the bus had slowed down and, at one point, actually seemed to pass right through them, although he did point out that he could have been mistaken.

A car-load of tourists who lost their way to Wetherby one day in 1968, found themselves on the same stretch of road. They noted what they considered to be six tramps stumbling silently along the ditch at the side of the country lane. Although they at first dismissed the group's unusual appearance as being drunken actors in 17th-century costume on their way home from a gala or fete, they changed their minds when they found that the expression on the men's faces was of dispiritedness and utter exhaustion rather than inebriation. The driver and passengers watched them for a while before driving on.

Vague folk tales of fantastical sights down the centuries sound remarkably similar at Marston Moor, with alleged witnesses describing Roundheads and Cavaliers desperately fighting it out, distant figures of weary travellers in battle-dress, and sudden glimpses of the battle silhouetted in the sky.

However, more recent sightings have been noted in the area, and the first case is probably the closest ever encounter with one of the old soldiers. In June 1991, Margaret and Dennis Howarth, of Hull, were driving to Cumbria to visit relatives, when they decided to take the longer but more scenic route and cut across Marston Moor. As there was little danger of crashing, with only the odd vehicle passing by, both Mrs Howarth at the wheel and her husband could cast frequent glances across the vast expanse of moorland, admiring its picturesque setting. Suddenly, Mr Howarth grabbed his wife's arm, and shouted for her to stop. Wincing, Mrs Howarth hurriedly slammed her foot on the brake pedal, bringing the car to an abrupt halt.

They both peered through the windscreen to see a man in a round metal helmet, which shone in the sunlight, crossing the road in front of their car. He did not react to the occupants in any way and, with his head bowed to the ground, continued on his way. Mr Howarth jumped out of the car and was about to remonstrate with him. Yet, in the time it took for him to climb out, the man had disappeared. His wife said that he had seemed to stoop down in the gully at the side of the road, so her angry husband went to look – but there was no sign of him. Both witnesses said that there was no way he could have hidden from them without being seen, simply because there was nowhere for him to go.

In 1995, also in the month of June, Derek Ainsley was returning from York, having just secured a business contract for his Lincolnshire-based company. Instead of keeping to the main road, he thought he would stop off for lunch at a village pub somewhere and, before he knew it, found himself on the moorland road.

He drove along, admiring the scenery, watching the sky grow darker. It looked like there would shortly be rain. As he continued on his way, the moors were rapidly engulfed in semi-darkness on this otherwise perfect summer afternoon. Momentarily, glancing through his driver's side window, he saw a lone figure ahead of him, trudging through the grass, in the same general direction. As the first drops of rain hit the windscreen, he gave another look at the sky, figuring the storm would last for a considerable time. Not being the sort of person who regularly offers lifts to pedestrians and hitch-hikers, he nevertheless decided to offer the person a ride, taking him to be a rambler and thinking that the storm would leave him drenched to the skin. With a crack of thunder from the sky, he stopped the car, wound down the window, and was about to shout across to the person. But there was no sign of him.

Confused, he turned his head to look back at the moors he had just passed on the same side of the road, and yet the figure simply wasn't there. Mr Ainsley didn't know what to think and, pausing for a few seconds for the rambler to reappear, he wound up his window and set off again.

Less than one minute later, and a few hundred yards further down the road, he saw what he took to be same person standing by the opposite side of the road. Mr Ainsley said that the figure, which he could now see was a man, was dressed in a long brownish cloak, with black knee-length boots, and was facing away from him. The man was wearing some kind of hat or cap but Mr Ainsley did not take much notice of it as the shock of seeing him again was just too great. There was no way the same person could have covered the 200 to

300 yards in so short a time and been able to cross the road and appear stationary at that point. It was just impossible!

This time, Mr Ainsley stopped as he drew level with the man, who did not acknowledge the arrival of the car, and leaned over to the passenger seat to wind down the window. As soon as he had done this, he found that the figure had gone. He did not see him vanish. Mr Ainsley told me it was simply as if he hadn't been there in the first place.

He grabbed his jacket from the back seat and climbed from the car to look for the man but could not see him anywhere. He thought he might have fallen down, unlikely though it may sound, but the grass was not particularly long at that spot and could not easily have concealed anyone. Then Mr Ainsley glanced back to the other side of the road, to where he had seen the original figure, but the only sight that met his gaze was isolated moorland becoming quickly drenched in the pouring rain.

Derek Ainsley can't offer an explanation for what he experienced. It wasn't scary – just intriguing – and it still puzzles him to this day.

7

The Grey Lady of Long Can

Constructed in 1637 by yeoman clothier James Murgatroyd, Long Can at Wheatley, Halifax, started out as a row of terraced cottages. Having stood derelict for many years there had been a number of proposals to demolish them but these were always denied because of the historical value of the property.

When the brewery Samuel Webster and Wilson's merged in the early 1980s, far from hiring a demolition team they invested money in a restoration project, with a view to using Long Can as the Brewery Visitors' Centre. They even employed some of Murgatroyd's own personal building techniques which he had used on other Yorkshire properties such as East Riddlesden Hall, in Keighley, to enhance the work. This turned out to be a worthwhile investment as Long Can won The Stone Federation 1987 Design Award for Natural Stone.

Unfortunately, during the restoration work, vandals broke into the building and set about wrecking all the hard work that had been put into it. However, for once, something good came from this mindless act. The wreckers inadvertently uncovered a hidden timber frame which was now visible beneath the plasterwork. Murgatroyd's own initials were carved into the wood with the date 1637, but 'J.M.S. 1708' was also evident, indicating that a later owner had made more alterations to the building 70 years on. Long Can's two-storey porch is evidence of Murgatroyd's 'architectural signature', and this was preserved along with other parts of the building such as the original diagonally-shaped floor.

After the restoration work began, and then after its completion, several unexplained incidents were recorded – suggesting, perhaps, that this is one more haunting which was 'unearthed' by building work (see the chapters concerning the cottage at Rastrick and the Stocksbridge Bypass).

Catering manageress Sarah Thornton told me of the eerie happenings she had experienced since starting work there in 1987. Among Ms Thornton's various duties at the visitors' centre, was preparing buffet lunches off the premises, then transporting them to the VIP suite on the top floor.

Ms Thornton said that though she always felt nervous when working alone in the building, this was usually the last thing on her mind as she busied herself setting the tables in one of the rooms upstairs. On one occasion, she heard the door open followed by footsteps leading to the adjoining room, and she rushed in to see who was there. On investigation, she found that the door was closed properly with no one in sight. She then hurried outside, calling to a security guard to accompany her until the guests arrived.

So sure that there was no rational explanation to account for it, she felt a little foolish telling the kitchen staff about the incident. To her surprise, the other members of staff came forward to tell of their own experiences of the resident ghost.

One waitress told Ms Thornton about the day she was browsing around the museum, also housed in Long Can, admiring the contents of a showcase. Suddenly, she was overcome with the feeling that someone was behind her and spun round to catch a glimpse of an elderly lady in a long grey dress who appeared to be falling downwards, as if through the floorboards. The waitress said she was shivering when she left the museum.

The host of Long Can, who is also in charge of the bar and cellar, heard about the staff's experiences and confided in them about his own. The thing that he most often noticed was the curious smell of eggs and bacon which often wafted through the bar and cellar area where he works, even when the kitchen was not in use. Later, he discovered that the cellar used to be the kitchen in the middle cottage before the conversion. Ghostly smells, it seems, are almost as common as visible figures and unearthly sounds: a licensee at the Grove Inn, Luddendenfoot, in Halifax, also told me of the frequent aroma of eggs and bacon and freshly-baked bread, when there is nothing to account for it.

Following a bank holiday, when Long Can was closed, the host returned to the Centre to find that the artefacts on display in the museum showcase had been moved from the top shelf to the bottom. They were not scattered but had been replaced neatly and in the same order in which they were originally placed. The objects could not have been moved without first unlocking and opening the glass door and moving them by hand. The only department to own a key was Security – and they hadn't touched it. These artefacts included a collection of old leather boots and shoes, which had been discovered behind an old fireplace during the renovation work. Research showed that they had been originally placed there because the occupants believed they would ward off evil spirits!

A former cleaner, Betty Greenwood, told how she had seen a white, opaque object glide past her and disappear through the door leading to the cellar, while she was working in the bar area. The temperature had suddenly dropped and she was inexplicably overcome with fright before the object appeared and flitted past her.

Another cleaner was working in the ladies' toilets when someone tapped her on the shoulder. She turned to find no one there and her colleague was still standing outside the toilets waiting for her.

Ms Thornton concluded that she felt very much at home at the lovely old building but when she is on her own, she rushes round to get her job finished because she senses that she is not alone.

8

The Haunting of Rastrick

IF THERE is one question which repeatedly poses itself to psychical researchers as they investigate allegedly haunted sites, it surely concerns the importance of stone. So numerous are the instances where residents have lived in comfortable and peaceful surroundings for years without even a hint of ghostly intrusion, only to have been alarmed to find their homes have suddenly taken in non-paying tenants as a result of a change in the building's stonework. It may sound like a joke, but it can be far from funny when one considers that a little restoration can cause so much disruption to one's household. Does stone really contain some special property which can soak up the atmosphere of one century, much like a sponge absorbs water, then drain it out, into another, when that material is disturbed?

When Marilyn and Peter Auty moved in to what was once two separate cottages on Thornhill Road, in Rastrick, Brighouse, in November 1974, little did they realise what effect a little restoration work would have. When interviewed by the local press, the couple described the apparition they had seen as a vague shape, resembling that of a monk in a cowled habit. They have also since described a figure Mr Auty saw as that of a Lady in Grey.

During a period when his wife was admitted to hospital, Mr Auty returned home one night at around 8 pm, prepared some supper and then sat down on the settee in the living room. Suddenly, he looked up to see a figure emerge from the kitchen door, of a woman in a grey cloak, which vanished near the front door. The odd thing he noticed was that the figure seemed to be cut off at the knees, which gave the effect that it was gliding rather than walking. This could be explained though, as the present floor had been raised by Mr Auty, a skilled joiner, some time after they moved in. The original flagged stone floor still existed, though at several inches below the new one. Whoever the mystery figure is, it is probably an earlier resident of the house, whose routine of crossing the paved floor from kitchen to front door was somehow captured in the structure of the house, thus playing back like a video film, every so often. Further evidence of the ghost being little more than a projection, rather than a living entity which could react to its new environment, is suggested by its lack of acknowledgement that it was being observed by Mr Auty at the time.

An interesting twist to the above incident concerns a fellow writer on the paranormal, Terence Whitaker who visited the Autys with his family in 1980, and made several attempts to take a photo of the couple standing close to the door where the ghost normally appears. Each time, Mr Whitaker's flash-gun failed, and it wasn't until the couple settled onto the settee that the equipment worked properly and the picture was taken.

Mrs Auty recalls an incident which occurred just after the Whitaker family had made their departure. She was in the lounge while her husband worked in the garden, when she heard someone call her name. She stood up and listened. It came again – this time more clearly and in a rather perturbed tone. Thinking her husband had had an accident, she rushed to the kitchen window to see he was still quite happily digging away in the garden. There had been no one else in the house.

Little is known about the site of the cottages, though they are thought to have been converted from an old inn dating as far back as 1690, which was itself built on a site of more ancient stock. If there is a ghostly monk on the premises, then this must be a much older apparition than that of the Grey Lady.

The Autys have experienced other phenomena in their home which may, or may not, be attributed to the Grey Lady. Mrs Auty says that the only time she has been afraid of the ghost was one night as she lay in bed with her eyes closed. She gradually became aware of someone or something behind her, leaning over the bed and breathing heavily. This experience lasted for an extremely uncomfortable half hour as she lay there, feigning sleep, not daring to roll over or open her eyes to see who or what was making the sounds.

Could the mystery phantom tell she was really awake? If not, then this may support the theory that ghosts appear independently – even when there is no one there to witness them. This idea seems to have some credence in this case, as neighbours of the couple have often reported a figure peering out through the bedroom window at the front of the cottage when the Autys are away on holiday, and the house is otherwise empty.

The wide range of incidents over the years has included the peculiar affair of the ornament bell, which stands on a shelf on the landing upstairs. Neighbours regularly rushed round in the small hours and banged on the door complaining about the sound of bell-ringing, which they insisted was emanating from the Autys' cottage even though the couple hadn't heard a thing. When this became a regular occurrence, the neighbours asked the couple to show them all the bells in the house and to ring each one in turn. Mrs Auty obliged – yet none of the bells sounded remotely like the noise they had heard, until she remembered the one they kept on the landing. The odd thing was that the clapper had been broken and lost by their visiting nephew some time ago, so Mrs Auty hit it with a pencil, and the neighbours felt sure that this was the bell that had awoken them each night!

One of their strangest experiences happened one day when Mrs Auty was getting ready to leave the house and catch the bus to town. Suddenly, she felt a sharp pain on the back of her head and the next thing she remembers was sitting on the floor wondering what had happened. When she went to catch the bus, a neighbour asked which one she was going to catch. When she told her, the neighbour gave her an odd look before telling her that Mrs Auty had missed it by a full 20 minutes. What had happened during that time? It remains a mystery to this day.

Much of the phenomena seem to centre around the staircase. It could be that this is the reason for the haunting as the staircase is a comparatively recent addition to the house – and replaced an old staircase which was knocked down when the previous owners vacated the premises. The Autys both feel that there may have been a room here at some point in the past, and several people including Mr Auty and his wife's sister feel that there is someone watching them when they are near to it. The latter, indeed, is so affected by the sensation that she flatly refuses to climb the stairs even when accompanied by someone.

The most regular ghostly occurrence in the Auty household is a 'swirling film of smoke' which usually appears around the staircase. This is the most baffling of phenomena as it just appears, in the air, and moves past the onlooker, then just as quickly vanishes. Mrs Auty first saw it after her husband had retired to bed one evening. She was tidying up downstairs, ready to retire herself when this filmy smoke appeared near the front door, stayed for a few seconds then disappeared again. The second time it appeared, Mrs Auty was vacuuming the stairs. She heard a persistent rapping, which sounded like someone tapping a coin on a pane of glass, so she went to the front door and then the back door to see who it was – only to find no one there. Confused, she climbed the stairs to continue her work and, as she neared the landing, watched the same filmy smoke appear at the side of the landing, glide straight across to the other side and then disappear.

That evening, at the dinner table, Mrs Auty began telling her husband what had happened that day. For a while, he listened politely, but his attention was suddenly drawn away, as he gazed over her shoulder. When she turned to follow his gaze, they both watched a very large and very old portrait on the wall behind them, visibly swinging from side to side, though there was no draught to account for it.

The Autys' experiences in the building over the years would be more than enough to send many people scampering into the sunset. However, they feel very much at home here and agree that the place has such a pleasant and welcoming atmosphere.

Mrs Auty told me that while they remain mystified by events that still happen in their home to this day, the ghost or ghosts are not threatening, unlike the antics of a poltergeist hurling things around the place. Whatever haunts their cottage appears to be quite friendly, and has not done them any damage. Indeed, they would be upset if it packed its bags and left to haunt someone else!

9

Radio-Active Ghosts

IT IS said that there are few people more sceptical of the paranormal than media personnel and, while they know it will always make a good story, they will often be the first to poke fun at the subject with a dismissive wave of the hand and a discreet snigger. Yet, amid the hustle and bustle of two BBC Yorkshire radio stations, with the staff working to tight deadlines to produce constant news reports and entertainment, there are a great many workers who refuse to laugh at ghost stories, with good reason.

Producers, presenters and administrators at BBC Radio Sheffield and BBC Radio Leeds have had numerous brushes with the supernatural, and when I enquired about their resident spooks, not only did they not snort and laugh derisively, but they came forward with their own experiences, and interviewed me on their programmes.

The building which now houses the Radio Sheffield studio is called Ashdell Grove on Westbourne Road, and has been described as one of the city's finest Victorian houses. Built in 1871 as Victoria Park, it was lived in by various prominent industrialists. In its time, it has been used as a private residence and a small hotel as well as by officers of the Red Cross, the Inland Revenue and Fire Brigade, and as a barrage balloon billet during the war.

There is a story to account for the alleged haunting, concerning a maid who committed suicide having been jilted by a local police constable with whom she was having an affair. However, as is often the case, the tale is rather vague, has not been corroborated by facts, and details seems to change depending on who is relating the account. Regardless of the origins of the ghost, there is a very definite presence here which certainly warrants further investigation and, busy though the staff are, they are friendly and approachable, and as interested as anyone to discover the reason for the haunting.

In March 1993, I was interviewed 'live' over the telephone by presenter Gerry Kersey, who was covering for comedian Tony Capstick while the latter was on vacation, as part of a programme about the staff's in-house ghost. Gerry often works alone at the studios at night and is used to the odd sounds, the clicks and the bumps, which can often be heard among the mass of electronic equipment stored there. However, one night as he walked past a cupboard on one of the upper floors he was amazed when the door burst open and a mass of tapes and spools flew out onto the floor. They didn't just fall out as they would have done had it been accidental, but it actually seemed as if they were being thrown out by someone inside – but, of course, there wasn't anyone there.

Another presenter staged a ghost-hunt one night, accompanied by psychic Graham Cheadle, and had some odd experiences. When the pair reached a small flight of steps, they both began to feel physically sick at the same time. Graham looked up to see the image of a tall man in his late forties standing motionless at the top of the stairs and staring down at them. The two men quickly recovered when they moved away from the immediate area. On another occasion, the same presenter was alone in the building, editing tapes until 2 am. Glancing up at the studio door, in which there is a square porthole, he swears he saw a shadow pass across the gap. He quickly stood up, dashed out into the passage and called out but, again, there was no one there.

Although many of these happenings could be put down to tricks of the light, or simply figments of the imagination, there have been too many people who experience the same sorts of things to dismiss everything that has occurred. Many have seen shadows and other images flitting past out the corner of their eye, while others have heard strange sounds and felt unseen presences. One young lady lived so far away from the studio that she decided to bed down on the studio floor one night. However, she found it difficult to settle, as she constantly felt there was someone watching her.

Senior Producer, Ralph Robinson, has walked out three times already. Twice because he, too, felt he was not alone, and once because strange things were happening to lights on electronic equipment which he simply couldn't explain away. In August 1988, former Sports Producer Phil Baldy, who had been working on the late news shift, walked to the door of the newsroom, which leads to the main staircase and archway, to see a vague, nondescript white object flutter across the archway. Quite unnerved, and deciding that enough was enough, he switched off all the studio lights and made his way to the glass-panelled door at the front of the building. He stepped outside and turned to lock it and, as he looked back, saw a face peering through the glass at him. At first he thought it was his own reflection, but the longer he looked he found it was the face of a strange old man staring back at him, at which point he became more than a little distressed and fled!

Footsteps have been heard by many members of staff including freelance reporter, Richard Hemmingway, who was alone in the newsroom one night. When he heard the front door open, and footsteps pass through the hall and up the corresponding flight of steps, he went to search the building but found no one. Later that same night, he also heard the unmistakable sound of lights being switched on and off.

The ghost or ghosts at BBC Radio Sheffield do not only put in appearances during the night; their pranks have been experienced in broad daylight too! Engineer Peter Mason was working alone in the newsroom one Sunday afternoon, listening to a news programme being broadcast at that time. He became aware that the volume was gradually diminishing, until the voices were barely audible. He rushed to the control room only to find that the volume knob had been deliberately turned down, even though there had been no one in the room at the time.

Although Ashdell Grove is a rambling old house with a welcoming and friendly atmosphere, the staff know from experience that there is something unseen and very real working alongside them.

Another team of radio broadcasters have had similar experiences at the headquarters of BBC Radio Leeds, at Broadcasting House on Woodhouse Lane. They share their building with what has been variously described as a Grey Lady or Lady in Black, and a strange hooded figure which prowls the premises.

In his book *Northcountry Ghosts and Legends*, author and broadcaster Terence Whitaker (who has also hosted 'ghost' programmes from haunted Studio 2 at Radio Lancashire in Blackburn) interviewed a former employee who worked at Radio Leeds during the Second World War. Albert Aldred recalled the years he worked there when he often heard footsteps pacing the notorious 'haunted gallery'. He noted that they always sounded as if they were walking on concrete rather than the carpeted floor which existed at the time. He also recalls that many members of staff did not like working there alone at night, and some even resigned from their jobs through fear.

When the BBC took over the building sometime in the 1930s, members of staff were constantly reporting the apparition of a hooded figure. It would often glide across the gallery into Studio 2, disappearing through the opposite wall.

Poltergeist activity had been experienced more recently by part-time receptionist Sharon Carter. One Sunday evening in December 1978, she had been sitting in the rest-room on the first floor talking to a friend on the telephone when the temperature suddenly dropped. She carried the phone to the sink where it seemed warmer and continued her conversation. A few moments later, she heard a resounding crash, as the lid of the kettle which had been placed on the floor near to where Sharon had been sitting, had turned itself round, floated up in the air and hurled itself at the sink! Sharon rushed from the room terrified and vowed never to return there. Other objects have been tampered with overnight. One reporter came into the newsroom one morning to find tapes and papers strewn across the room, and a typewriter turned upside down on a desk.

Former producer Caroline Woodruff has been among the many staff who have hurriedly vacated the premises at night, particularly in the notorious Studio 2, on being overcome with the unnerving sensation of being watched by unseen eyes.

When contacting BBC Radio Leeds, not only was I helped with my research but the producers arranged to do a Ghost Report for their *Saturday Breakfast Show*. It was a curious experience being interviewed on the radio, 'live' over the telephone, but very interesting. I was advised to turn off my radio, because it would cause interference on the telephone line during the interview, and at 8.45 am, I could hear the report beginning. Cue 'spooky music', and the interviewer's voice echoing through the microphone as if he was sitting in a haunted dungeon somewhere. The report began with a journalist interviewing various members of staff who have claimed to experience the ghost.

Although no one has actually seen the ghost recently, the presence is a very real phenomenon experienced by countless people. One lady who works at the station talked of the presence and how she often felt nervous in the vicinity of Studio 2. Another lady said that she often played the piano in the studio during her breaks, and that she could always hear a strange sound, as if someone was humming or whistling along to the music. When she stops playing to listen to the sound it will continue for a few seconds before ceasing – then begin again when she continues. Another employee, one of many who refrained from giving their names, told how he always took the long way round when he was the first to arrive in the morning, consciously steering clear of spooky Studio 2.

So if nothing has been seen – is it all in the mind? Another programme for BBC Radio Leeds the following May again had me as a 'guest' on the telephone, along with medium Julie Cryer, presenter Liz Green and various listeners ringing in with their own experiences. The programme began with a pre-taped interview with noted sceptic Dr Susan Blackmore who said she was convinced that so-called paranormal phenomena are not a physical reality. However, more accounts were forthcoming about the Radio Leeds ghost, which are not easy to dismiss because of the number of different people whose experiences tally in detail. Sarah Thomas, who has worked at the building for over 18 years, said that when she first started work there, many older members of staff told of how they had seen a ghostly figure pacing the notorious gallery, which looks onto Studio 2 and acts as a thoroughfare to the newsroom.

When the March interview was drawing to a close I added, half-jokingly, that it would be a good idea for me to spend a night in Studio 2 with a video camera – to see if I could catch anything tangible on film.

The presenter gave a nervous laugh and said: 'Rather you than me, Andy!'

10

'Who Ya Gonna Call?'

Most people who are lucky or unlucky enough to find themselves living in a haunted house usually just have that one experience. Either they vacate the premises, or seek help from spiritualist mediums, or rid themselves of their unwanted guests in one way or another – and never experience anything like that again. However, for one man this has not been possible.

Graham Cheadle was born on 7th May 1941 at a house situated in Heeley, in Sheffield, which was definitely haunted. Soon after, the family moved to a property at Hastiler Road South which, again, had a spectral lodger. In fact, five of the houses he has resided in over the course of his life have contained some form of psychic presence.

In February 1994, Graham had been a divorced man for six years and, deciding to remedy this state of affairs, he answered an advertisement in the lonely hearts column of a local paper. Jean, a widow, soon got in touch and they found they enjoyed each other's company so much that they married the same year on 14th July.

Jean still treasured fond memories of her first husband Alan, who had died ten years previously, and Graham would often accompany her to the cemetery in Hatfield Woodhouse, near Doncaster, to place flowers there. On one of the visits, Graham secretly promised Alan that he would take care of Jean and, it seems, Alan returned to make sure Graham stuck to his word!

Soon after they married, Graham and Jean moved into a house on Dryden Road, in the Southy Green area of the city, and it wasn't long before they had some odd experiences. The strong smell of tobacco smoke was evident in various parts of the house, even though neither of them smoke; electrical appliances, like the TV, satellite receiver and water supply to the washing machine, would regularly switch themselves off; and doors would open and close during the night. One of the most curious occurrences concerned their bearded collie, Ben. The couple would often hear him jumping up and down and frantically pulling his lead in the hallway where he slept during the night.

At the time, neither Graham nor Jean realised it was Alan who was responsible for the ghostly goings-on. However, as the weird happenings began to escalate, Graham thought it was time to seek some expert help and put a stop to the disturbances.

During July 1995, he was listening to the radio and caught the last few minutes of a programme about 'ghosts' and a group of Sheffield bus drivers, from the Mainline bus company, who had formed a psychic research group. As a result of this, Graham contacted the radio station and subsequently appeared on the programme *Roney & Steph's Breakfast Show* together with three of the ghost-hunters from Mainline. Graham recounted how it seemed that Ben had found an invisible playmate and the odd behaviour of the electrical equipment. The ghost-hunters listened patiently, then said they thought they could help Graham and Jean with their problem, and arranged to visit the house a few days later to 'see what they could find'.

When they arrived they requested freedom of the house, and proceeded to move from room to room making both mental and written notes about various 'psychic vibrations' they could feel. About one hour later, they all met up in the sitting room to compare notes and discuss what they had sensed. Much to the couple's surprise, the visitors went on to describe a man of Alan's appearance, which was exact down to the very last detail, including his stature, his beard and his occasional pipe-smoking habit.

One of the group, Gary, asked Jean if she wanted Alan to 'pass on to the higher realms' and, having taken a moment to compose herself, Jean replied that she did. The group sat in silent prayer and meditation for some time to allow the spiritual door to open and give Alan access to the next stage of life. Gary then gave Jean some spiritual healing, and a couple of minutes later, two members of the group described how they 'saw' Alan move to Jean, then to Graham, as if to say 'goodbye' to them both – and then he was gone.

Graham and the Ghostwatch Group, as they came to be known, returned to the radio programme and recounted their story in a special follow-up report to the original show. And that, it seemed, was that.

In September 1994, Graham and Jean decided it was time for a change of scenery and arranged a house exchange with a young couple and their two young sons from the Arbourthorne Estate, in Sheffield. Graham said that he should have known better, based on past experience, but the exchange went ahead, and they subsequently discovered why the family had been so very eager to move.

The first week in October saw Graham, Jean and Ben settling down in their new home – a very large two bedroomed house, near a derelict cinema. The house had been built in the 1960s, constructed on the site of a former house dating from just before the Second World War.

Everything was fine until Christmas, when Jean's grandchildren came to stay for the holidays. Initially, the TV started to go haywire again, this time changing channels on its own, which became very frustrating for the couple. The remote control handsets were always placed on the coffee table, and when the channels switched no one was anywhere near them. Also, the scent of perfume of a variety that Jean did not use was frequently evident and, again, the occasional whiff of pipe tobacco could be smelled. This immediately made Graham think of Alan, but this was not the case.

A few weeks into the New Year, Graham began to feel a strange 'coldness' at the top of the stairs near the landing, and it was this sensation especially which became stronger and stronger over the next few weeks until it was quite overpowering. Graham always knew he had been psychically susceptible to the paranormal and often experienced things which he could never fully explain, and it was during this period that he was somehow 'told' about their visitor. He occasionally received the impression of a lady named Ann, who was around 5'6" in height, with long blonde hair down to her shoulders. Graham never got used to this ability and he began to feel very wary at the thought of experiencing the cold spot on the stairs every night. Eventually, he and Jean decided it was time to call the Ghostwatch Group again.

By this time, Graham had become a member of the Group and when the team arrived he told them about all the vibrations he had been experiencing from their new visitor. When the Group went to work Graham found he had been correct in the name and appearance of the lady. Her name *was* Ann, and she appeared of average height with long blonde hair. When the Group made contact she explained that she had been murdered by her mother, and the Group subsequently contacted her mother's spirit which was also in the house. After much communication, the Group reunited the presences of Ann and her mother and released them from their earthbound state. The Group had achieved yet another success.

Graham and Jean were hoping that this was the last ghostly encounter they would ever experience in this house or anywhere else for that matter, but there was one more little problem to deal with first. After Ann and her mother had passed on, Graham began to see the image of a little boy. The images began to get stronger and more frequent and he met him one night on the landing as Graham was leaving the bathroom. The boy followed Graham into the bedroom and stood beside Jean who was still fast asleep.

The boy told Graham his name was Peter, and now that 'all the others had gone' he had been left on his own with no one to talk to, and he asked Graham to help him. Graham promised Peter he would do everything in his power to help and knew that once again it was time to call the Ghostwatch Group.

Gary and Cynthia from the Ghostwatchers called round to see if they could help, and both agreed that the presence was of a young boy and confirmed that his name was Peter. However, Gary also picked up sensations of another soul, an even younger boy, which Peter had been unaware of at the time. The younger boy, aged about two and a half, turned out to be Peter's younger brother who was inextricably linked with Peter and could therefore not leave this world.

The Group learned that one day, many years ago when the two boys were still alive, Peter had been playing with a metal spinning-top. As he swung it round in the air it accidentally hit his younger brother on the side of the head, killing him instantly. Although it had been an accident, Peter's father never forgave his eldest son, and as a result, Peter was so full of remorse that he took his own life. Peter drowned himself one day in a small fishing pond at Arbourthorne, which still exists today and has been there since the mid-1800s. Peter's suicide marked a double tragedy for his parents and the emotional anguish they must have gone through would have been virtually indescribable. As Gary and Cynthia directed the boys towards the Light, another figure emerged to meet them: the boys' father, who came to take his sons with him. And then, it was over.

In a postscript to Graham's account, he explained that there is still a little paranormal activity occurring inside a house on Algar Road from where they moved in October 1997. Unfortunately, he was unable to ascertain exactly who or what the presence was – either male or female – and it seemed somehow reluctant to make its presence fully known to him. It is interesting to note that, whatever is at the root of the disturbances, it does not seem to be content with just one home. Neighbours on either side of the property have been experiencing identical phenomena.

However, although Graham considered that he and Jean had left it all behind, he points out that the Ghostwatch Group seem to have quite a lot of work to do in the future. And not just in their former house. The sound of footsteps from the bathroom, when there is no one else in the house, could be the start of another fascinating adventure.

And if that's the case – who are they gonna call . . . ?

Close Encounters of a Deadly Kind

AT 3.30 PM on the sunny afternoon of Friday 6th June 1980, Zigmund Adamski set off from his home in Wakefield to the local shops – and vanished off the face of the earth. That was the last time anyone saw him alive, for his body was found in a coal hopper, five days later and 25 miles away in the market town of Todmorden.

How he got there, how he died, where he had been in the missing days, baffled everyone who investigated the mystery – and it remains unsolved to this day. In fact, there are those who believe it will never be explained – at least not in so-called 'rational' terms.

However, to examine this mystery we must first look at the events leading up to the disappearance.

Zigmund Jan Adamski was Polish by birth and, like so many of his fellow countrymen, he had settled in England having been forced to flee his country during the war. He set up home in the West Yorkshire village of Tingley, became a coal miner and, in 1951, married Leokadia or 'Lottie'. When she became so ill that she was confined to a wheelchair, Zigmund needed to spend more time with her. His own health, too, was under question, and he had been off work for several months; a lung deformity often made breathing difficult – and it was with this extra factor that Zigmund decided to apply for early retirement. This was rejected, but his company's decision was reviewed quite soon after and the application subsequently accepted. Unfortunately, the reversed decision arrived in the post the day after he disappeared.

Upsetting though this was, family and friends were sure he had not gone missing through depression. He would never have left his wife; neighbours spoke of how devoted the couple were to each other.

On the day that Adamski disappeared, he had been shopping in Wakefield town centre with his cousin and her son who were visiting the Adamskis from Poland. That afternoon, the trio returned to the couple's home and sat down to a fish and chip dinner. Adamski was enjoying his cousin's visit and was also very excited about the next day; he was due to give away his god-daughter in marriage. He had a speech specially prepared for the occasion, and would not have let the couple down for any reason.

At half-past three, Adamski announced that he would pop out to the local shop just a few hundred yards down the street to buy some potatoes. He grabbed his jacket containing wallet, driving licence and some small change, and left the house. Passing a few desultory comments with a neighbour washing his car, he set off to the shops – but never reached them.

When Adamski did not return home that evening, Lottie contacted Wakefield police to report his disappearance, but despite intensive police enquiries and an appeal in local newspapers, their investigations drew a blank. That is, until almost exactly five days later to the minute, when his body was discovered.

At 3.45 pm, on Wednesday 11th June 1980, Trevor Parker, the son of a Todmorden coal merchant, arrived at his father's yard to find a man's body resting in a hollow at the top of a pile of coal. He had already been there that morning at 8.15 and was quite sure that the body was not there at that time. In the intervening hours, while Mr Parker had been absent, the gates of the yard had been left unlocked just in case any deliveries arrived. As it happens there had been none.

Mr Parker was understandably astonished to find the body, and he stood rooted to the spot for a while before composing himself and phoning for an ambulance. It was not only the fact that he had found the man here at all that was odd, for there were several other unaccountable points. It would have been a difficult task for a man to climb up the greasy side of the coal pile, even more so because it had been raining for most of the day, and Zigmund would have found it almost impossible because of his breathing problems. The dead man was wearing his jacket, but his shirt was missing; and Mr Parker had noticed a strange burn mark on the back of the man's head, neck and shoulder, which he would not touch.

Twenty-five minutes later, police officers Mervyn Haig and Alan Godfrey arrived to inspect the body and to question Mr Parker. The latter told them what he knew, but there seemed to be nothing which could throw light on the mystery. The body was transferred to the mortuary at nearby Hebden Bridge and, that night at 9.15 pm, a post-mortem was conducted by a consultant pathologist, to ascertain the cause of death.

From his examination, Dr Alan Edwards estimated that the time of death was between 11.15 am to 1.15 pm – around eight to ten hours prior to the post-mortem. The body, therefore, had been in the yard for at least two and a half hours before its discovery. No major physical injuries were evident – certainly no internal injuries – which showed he had probably not died from an assault of any kind. There were, however, the curious oval-shaped burn marks on the left of the neck and also below the ear. These had caused a slight loss of skin, brown discolouration and a tacky substance had been applied to them, presumably a form of ointment. Dr Edwards thought that the marks indicated contact with a corrosive substance but he could not ascertain what it was. Although the burns were not minor injuries he was sure they were not the cause of death. They could have caused some alarm to Adamski and brought on a heart attack. The final verdict was 'natural causes', as he had obviously died from heart and chest disease.

Even though Zigmund Adamski was found minus his shirt (which was never recovered) he had not been sleeping rough. His body showed that he had only one day's growth of stubble – so he had evidently been staying somewhere and, even though his stomach was empty, this merely indicated that he had not eaten on the day of his death. Dr Edwards found an abrasion on the man's right thigh, and superficial cuts on both of his hands and knees.

UFOlogist Jenny Randles, who has written more than 20 books on UFOs and the paranormal, including the Pennine UFO Mystery, points out that everyone who has investigated the case remains quite baffled.

The Pennine UFO Mystery is a down-to-earth investigation about a number of separate events that mainly occurred between June and November 1980, which the media linked together in a fantastic 'UFO' story. While Ms Randles does not for one minute suggest that UFOs were responsible for the disappearance and subsequent reappearance and death of Zigmund Adamski, she does not dismiss the idea, either, sensibly leaving the reader to decide. While the UFO theory seems wildly improbable, it is pertinent, I think, to include the reasons why the Adamski death was initially linked to this phenomenon.

In the weeks leading up to the disappearance, there had been numerous reports to newspapers and the police about orange fireballs and other unidentified flying objects seen across West Yorkshire, mainly in Bradford, Halifax and Todmorden. While some of these sightings were explained away as aircraft, atmospheric phenomena, and flares used by moorland rescue teams, some remained unexplained, including quite a substantial amount which were reported *after* Adamski had disappeared.

In addition, one of the two police officers who arrived at the coalyard on 11th June allegedly had a close encounter with a UFO.

During the early morning of Friday 28th November 1980, policeman Alan Godfrey, who was on night patrol, was driving along Burnley Road, which leads out of Todmorden, when he saw a huge object with a spinning top section and a row of windows, hovering above the road ahead of him. He stopped the car 100 yards away from the UFO and attempted to contact the police station on both his car radio and mobile 'walkie-talkie', but he could not get through. The next thing he knew, he was 100 yards further down the road from where he had been and, although he didn't realise it at that moment, there had been a substantial time-lapse. Eventually, with advise from MUFORA (the Manchester UFO Research Association) he agreed to be hypnotised to discover what had happened during that missing time, of which he had no recollection. The subsequent hypnosis session brought to light PC Godfrey's astounding account of being taken inside the UFO and examined by alien beings, which seemed to have been buried in his subconscious and erased from conscious memory.

Whether or not this has any connection with the Adamski death is not known, but all investigators have been unable to find a conventional solution to the mystery. There are several reasons why Adamski was connected to the UFO theory. He had obviously been somewhere during those five days – but no one had reported seeing him, and the way his body reappeared was very odd. It was found in broad daylight on top of a coal pile without easy access, and in the vicinity of a busy railway line. No one had reported seeing anything odd during those hours; any effort to place the body in that particular location would have been a hard and cumbersome task, almost certainly resulting in footmarks or some form of indentations in the coal and immediate vicinity. And it would have been a foolhardy and pointless objective for anyone wanting to dispose of a body in the first place. The idea that he had simply dropped from the sky seemed as likely a theory as any.

We should also consider, however, where and when he went missing. Had Zigmund Adamski disappeared during the hours of darkness it would be quite understandable – many hundreds of people go missing at night – but it was early Friday afternoon in late spring when Adamski set off on his errand, and so it seems even more astonishing that no one saw him after that point. The fact that he never reached the shop obviously means that something happened to him on the way there. But what? Even if the UFO abduction theory was considered as a serious alternative, it would still sound implausible in light of this factor alone. What did they do? Beam him up in broad daylight – like Scotty does in *Star Trek*?

Zigmund Adamski has been described as a loving family man, with no known enemies. Although dogged by bad health, he had a lot to live for. Here was a man who had been a prisoner of war, escaped the horror of the Nazis, settled and married and worked in England, only to die in the most mysterious of circumstances.

I have included the mystery here with all the best intentions. Certainly not to cause more grief to the family of the deceased, but in the hope that one day an answer will be forthcoming. Perhaps a reader of this volume will take up the challenge and throw new light on what has been dubbed Yorkshire's mystery of the century?

12

Poltergeist: The Invisible Intruder

MORE and more people are becoming greatly interested in the subject which we currently term 'the paranormal'. While this almost certainly has much to do with television series like *The X-Files*, not to mention the almost apprehensive attitude to the new Millennium, general public awareness that such things are worthy of serious scientific investigation is constantly on the increase.

In the early 1980s, with the founding of various small paranormal investigation societies, there seemed to be a need for a much larger society which could act as 'umbrella' for these small groups. The idea that researchers from all corners of the nation, indeed the world, regardless of their own personal beliefs, could join a totally non-biased association in which ideas, news, and advice could be exchanged, was a worthy and challenging one.

On 10th June 1981, ASSAP (the Association for the Scientific Study of Anomalous Phenomena) was formed to provide this much-needed forum. One of their aims was to provide the resources to train people to become investigators, so that cases could be researched, people interviewed, evidence recorded and new knowledge about the paranormal made available.

Poltergeists are one of the subject areas ASSAP investigators are trained to deal with. A specially-appointed National Investigations Co-ordinator has a network of trained investigators at his fingertips, and accordingly co-ordinates cases to be investigated as and when they are reported. One such case of poltergeist activity, however, came straight to the attention of experienced investigator Colin

Davies, and he set about recording the phenomena on video. As ASSAP operate a strict code of ethics, to protect witnesses from unwanted media publicity and public ridicule, confidentiality about real names and actual locations has to be adopted.

Poltergeist activity had been regularly experienced in what we shall call The Bed Shop, in Yorkshire, and the manager only agreed to the investigation under strict confidentiality. Indeed, the activity had already cost him a fair amount of business from customers, as we shall see. I am indebted to ASSAP's Executive Committee for allowing me to include details of 'The Yorkshire Poltergeist', which are also available on their Internet web-site, and to Colin Davies for writing such a lucid account of his investigation.

Colin first heard about the case from his brother Mike who was working in a carpet shop just a few doors away from The Bed Shop. Their sister-in-law and her husband had visited the shop in question in the hope of buying a new bed. They were standing alone on the first floor of the showroom, and were understandably shocked when some coins came flying at them from nowhere and just missed them. There was no one else on that first floor at the time, and they rushed down to tell the proprietor. The man was not surprised. 'Don' told them that this had been going on for a couple of months now, and he was quite willing to explain the situation to Mike, when he called round during his lunch break.

Don related how coins, pens, staplers and other objects would often fly through the air when there had been no one around to throw them. Items had gone missing from offices, only to reappear a few days later, often in the original places they had been. Also some of the missing items would materialise in mid-air and just drop to the floor. However, the next point was particularly interesting. When an object appeared and dropped to the floor it would always hit something that would make a sound, like a cardboard box or the metal strip which joined two carpets together.

On the day of his first visit after Mike had passed on this information, on Saturday 10th November 1990, Colin felt an 'incredible shiver' running through him, and knew something was about to happen. He watched as a marker pen suddenly appeared a few centimetres below the ceiling. It proceeded to fly across the shop, closely hugging the ceiling for about three metres, then arch downwards, hitting a cardboard box. Colin said it felt as if all his hairs were standing on end – and what a pity the camcorders he had brought with him were not yet up and running!

Colin was present during many of the subsequent occurrences, when no one else was with him. He watched items, such as keys, flying around the office, hitting filing cabinets, and dropping to the floor. He also heard a 'ping' sound on one of the cabinets and, on investigation, found a cigarette lighter had just appeared there. A few seconds later, Don came into the office. He said that he had used his lighter to light a customer's cigarette, then put it down and it had disappeared. He was amazed when Colin handed it to him!

Both Don and his assistant 'Susie' had been present when loud thumps had been heard from unoccupied upper floors. Lights had been switched on and off; keys, marker pens, coins, and other items had flown across the room, missing people by inches; and all these things had been witnessed by a number of the shop staff and a delivery man. A price tag reading £654 was found in the office where it should not have been. In addition, one number had been switched round, to read £954. Don re-arranged the number, took it upstairs and placed it on the bed where it should have been. Just a few minutes later, he found the tag had disappeared, and he later found it back in the office, reading £954 again!

The word poltergeist comes from two German words: Polter meaning 'noisy' or 'racket' and Geist meaning 'ghost' or 'spirit'. In view of some the above activities, the theory that poltergeists are noisy ghosts would seem to be a fair interpretation – and the making of a noise with each activity suggests that the agent responsible for the disturbance was constantly trying to get attention for some reason. While spiritualists say that poltergeists are, indeed, ghosts attempting to be noticed and it is often the case that visual apparitions and poltergeist activity occur at the same location, there has been another theory proposed in recent years.

Psycho-kinesis, denoting the power of the mind over physical objects (eg: spoon-bending by Uri Geller), could be responsible for poltergeists. In a television programme screened in 1998, ASSAP Investigations Officer Phillip Walton pointed out that 'stress' was the one common denominator in most outbreaks of poltergeist activity. Could it be that people who are troubled, for one reason or another, could inadvertently have an effect on the immediate environment?

Colin says that in most cases of poltergeists there is a focus – a person around whom the activities revolve. The focus is usually an adolescent or, indeed, someone suffering from stress. Don's assistant 'Susie' was certainly that focus in this case, as she had been suffering from considerable stress at the time. Colin had the idea that if he left a camcorder switched on in the office with her, while convincing her he had switched it off, then perhaps the poltergeist would also believe it and begin performing again.

Colin therefore left one of his camcorders running in the office, facing in Susie's direction. He told Susie that he would switch off the camera because nothing seemed to happen when it was on. Susie thought it worth a try, and although Colin switched it off by the mains supply, he kept it on, powered by an internal battery. The camera was making a noise, and the lens cap was off, which seemed to make Susie a little nervous, though Colin fibbed and told her the noise was just the sound of the battery running down after use. He explained, 'It was just the best excuse I could think of on the spur of the moment!'

Susie accepted this explanation, and Colin left her alone with the camera. In the course of the next 20 minutes he could hear various knocks and raps coming from the office. Some time later, he returned to pick up the camera, then took it home and rewound the tapes. On checking the VHS tape, it was obvious that Susie had been responsible for some of the knocks – she could be seen kicking her leg against the wooden wall in front of her desk. But she did not make all of the sounds. Out of the 14 sessions of recording, three were completely blank although there should have been no reason for this to happen. In addition, one taped session was visually recorded but with no sound. The camera had not developed a fault. Indeed, the equipment did not possess the ability to film a scene and isolate the microphone. The poltergeist had achieved the impossible!

During the course of the next week, Colin received in excess of 70 'strange' phone calls. Sometimes there were electronic bleeps on the other end, sometimes just silence. On a number of occasions his answerphone recorded Don saying, 'Hello, The Bed Shop, can I help you?' Curiously, when he asked Don about this, Don had had similar calls on his phone; again, sometimes just silence, and other times he would receive Colin's answerphone message. Apparently, both phones were being called simultaneously by each other! An enquiry to British Telecom drew a blank; they could provide no explanation.

When Colin next visited the premises, Don told him he was getting fed up with the poltergeist messing about with the business phones. He kept getting cut off when talking to customers and he was anxious about the probable loss of business it was causing. He decided to call on the services of the local vicar to perform an exorcism, to take place on Monday 3rd December 1990.

The day arrived and the exorcism was attended by Don, Susie, Colin, and two of Don's employees, Scott and Norman, and performed by a Church of England vicar, the Rev Peter Brown, and an assistant, Ben. Rev Brown said prayers and blessings over each individual present and the 'evil spirit' was commanded to be gone from each and every room in the building. He told Don that everything would now return to normal, though a second visit might be required in the future.

Unfortunately, some days later, Don phoned Colin to say that things were more or less as they had been before the exorcism. There were also messages written in the office and toilet areas. Two messages were 'BRING COLIN BACK NEED TO TALK WITH HIM CONTACT (Colin's telephone number)' and 'DON BRING HIM BACK THEN BROWN'.

The next time Colin visited, Don showed him reams of paper with messages written on them including 'COLIN IS COMING TODAY'. A particularly interesting one was found just before one of Colin's visits, 'HE IS AT CARPET SHOP (telephone number) I THINK RING HIM YOU HAVE TO TELL HIM B4 I WILL GO'. Strangely, Colin had just been to visit his brother Mike at the carpet shop, a few doors away, before arriving at The Bed Shop, and the telephone number was that of Mike's carpet shop. How did it know where Colin had been?

Colin Davies concludes his report with a postscript in which he says that the activity eventually died away. Even though he didn't catch it on film his observation of the marker pen which hugged the ceiling for a distance of about three metres, was incredible. Thrown objects move in a parabola, as the momentum decreases and they drop to the floor, while on this occasion it just moved horizontally on a constant. The strange happenings with the phones were also interesting, though he points out that we can only have the word of telecommunications engineers that such things are impossible. Interestingly, similar instances of interference with telephones have been noted in later cases which Colin investigated for ASSAP. Also interesting, is how Susie 'manufactured' some of the phenomena as certain witnesses often feel compelled to do, when the 'real thing' does not perform to order.

Colin's conclusion states that certain incidents in this case, such as the flying pen, which he personally witnessed, make it highly likely that the paranormal was responsible for a good proportion of the incidents witnessed.

Would you like to join ASSAP? For details of membership, please contact the Registered Office at 20 Paul Street, Frome, Somerset, BA11 1DX. ASSAP is a registered charity (number 327422) and a company limited by guarantee.

13

Knightly Ghosts at Middleham

O<small>NCE</small> known as the 'capital of Wensleydale', the village of Middleham lies nine miles south of Richmond, in North Yorkshire.

At the top of the main street stands Middleham Castle, some of it thought to date from 1068, since the time of Alan the Red – a stout supporter of William I. Middleham is well-known as the birthplace of Richard of Gloucester, later to become Richard III. It was previously owned by Richard Neville, the Earl of Warwick. The Victorian novelist, Lord Lytton, wrote of the castle and its notable guests: 'The most mightiest peers, the most renowned knights, gathered to his [Warwick's] hall. Middleham – not Windsor nor Sheen, nor Westminster, nor the Tower – seemed the court of England.' It was later forfeited to the crown when Warwick was killed in the Battle of Barnet in 1471. Imprisoned at Middleham during the Wars of the Roses, Edward IV subsequently passed it on to his brother, Richard III.

Some parts of this beautiful castle were destroyed by Cromwell, during the Civil War, but other parts remain standing, most notably the impressive Norman keep, with its walls measuring four yards thick. By the end of the 19th century, it had become nothing more than a ruin – and a dangerous one at that – and such it remained until the Ministry of Works restored some of the building in the 1920s. Currently in the care of English Heritage, the castle is open to the public for most days of the week, and well worth a visit.

It seems that most castles throughout Britain boast some sort of ghostly legend of one form or another. Tales of gallant knights, and damsels in distress abound in glossy tourist brochures, along with the odd dragon or two thrown in for good measure – and why not indeed? Everyone likes a lively, colourful tale which reflects the history, though maybe not wholly accurately, of a historic property such as a castle, which has borne witness to so many notable personages and events. And many of these ghostly tales, eccentric traditions or customs, like all folklore, have a basis, albeit a small basis, in truth. Middleham, however, is one of the few castles, along with Dover Castle, in Kent, and Windsor Castle, where modern accounts of the paranormal are still reported today.

English Heritage staff, custodians of the castle, and many visitors have seen and heard odd things in recent years. Indeed, one retired Anglican priest claims to have had actual spirit communication, through a medium, with Richard III himself.

I had an interesting telephone conversation with Reverend John Dening, Honorary Chaplain to the Society of Friends of Richard III, and author of his fascinating study *Secret History: The Truth about Richard III and the Princes* (Plantagenet Press, 1996). Although he is obviously fascinated by the history of the Plantagenet prince, with his interest extending into the realms of psychical research and the afterlife, he is not in the slightest bit 'cranky'. Indeed, a more down-to-earth chap you would be hard pushed to find.

The first he heard about the supposed haunting at Middleham was from a colleague, Mannie Norman, the secretary and general organiser of the group, who had been strolling around the castle grounds one weekend evening during the May Day Bank Holiday of 1991. Ms Norman and two friends clearly heard strange, old-fashioned music emanating from somewhere in the ruins, and they excitedly told the rest of the Society members. With his interest aroused, Rev Denning and five colleagues, including the Society's chairman, Dick Boustred, arranged to go for a prowl around the ruins on the third night of their visit to Middleham, to see if the experience could be repeated.

Some time had elapsed as the group walked through the almost completely dark environs of the castle, and as they came to a halt on the south side of the castle near the entrance to the Great Hall, Ms Norman suddenly whispered for them to listen. As the group strained their ears they all became aware of the sound of music. Ms Norman said that it was exactly what she and her friends had heard on the first occasion.

Rev Denning told me they were all fascinated as they listened to what he described as 'olde-world music of an early Renaissance type', which came floating over the night air, seemingly from somewhere near the north side of the castle. They listened intently for about half a minute, until it faded away. A few minutes later, similar snatches of the same type of music were heard again, until all was silent. Rev Denning points out another odd thing. Each snatch of music was accompanied by the sound of a dog barking from the same direction – though the group did not hear it either before or after the music played.

Rev Denning was not entirely convinced that there was anything even remotely supernatural about the music and thought there must, somehow, be a rational explanation. He admits to being really quite startled when, just 15 minutes later, at about 11 pm, the same music started up again. They were still standing outside the Great Hall, though this time it seemed considerably nearer and louder than before. However, although louder, the music still seemed to be vaguely muffled as if it was being played behind great doors, somewhere inside the castle.

Rev Denning points out that there was clearly no question of a hoax, and various explanations were suggested by the group of six – and subsequently dismissed – before retiring that night. He added that it was not a frightening experience at all, just intriguing. So intriguing that he returned the following year (May Day Bank Holiday, 1992) with the psychical research group of which he is a member to hold a vigil. Although they were hoping to record something on their sophisticated equipment, unfortunately – perhaps inevitably, he says – they did not hear a thing.

Rev Denning heard another first hand experience from the

summer of 1991, from someone he describes as a surprisingly serious-minded boy aged ten who lived in a cottage close to the castle. The clergyman was sitting on the grass outside the South Wall, under the rounded (Prince's) Tower, when the boy approached him and they got into conversation about the castle. The Reverend mentioned the incident of the ghostly music. The boy seemed particularly glad to have found someone to tell his own story to – someone who would listen seriously to what he had to say.

He and two friends who had been staying with his family were walking along that very path on the edge of the field on the south side one night. It was nearly dark and the three were excitedly discussing their plans for the next day. Suddenly, in the gathering gloom, a knight appeared sitting astride a horse right in front of them. Without warning, he charged clean through them at full pelt before they even had the chance to stand aside! Dazed and confused, they looked back to where the knight should have been – but he was nowhere to be seen. Barely had they time to recover from this shock when they distinctly heard for about ten or fifteen seconds the sound of clashing metal, like sword-on-sword, from somewhere near at hand inside the castle ruins. Rev Denning said that the boy had a very real air of conviction about him, and the latter claimed no additional psychic experiences before that event.

Other incidents have been noted, collected by the Reverend Denning from society members, not to mention ASSAP Investigator Chris Huff's interviews with staff who work at the castle.

Mannie Norman had a more recent experience one evening while standing nearly at the same spot where the music had been heard, accompanied by a young Irish lady, a fellow member of the society. They both watched a strange and seemingly inexplicable blue light appear at the top of the South Wall, and the young lady promptly fled in abject terror! Mannie, however, stood her ground, and watched as the light slowly descended to the foot of the wall, where it vanished.

The Society's research officer, Mrs Margaret Walker, was standing under the archway at the main entrance on the north side of the castle when she heard the very distinct sound of horses' hooves, 'clip-clopping' very close at hand. It must be said that the countryside around Middleham is well-known as an area where horses are trained and exercised regularly, but upon immediately checking for 'flesh and blood' horses in the vicinity, Mrs Walker drew a complete blank.

However, Rev Denning points out that perhaps the most intriguing of all sightings occurred around 1987, when former custodian of the castle, Sue Constantine was approached by a mother and her son who were visiting the ruins. The young boy had asked his mother if she thought 'the soldier' would be kind enough to show him his sword.

'What soldier?' asked his mother. Of course, she could see no one.

Even as I write, various psychical research groups, including ASSAP who have compiled a gazetteer of sightings for research purposes, are planning 'vigils' or ghost-hunts to Middleham.

And for any reader wishing to stage their own attempt, the ruins of Middleham Castle are perhaps one of the most fruitful places to start!

14

The White Lady of the Whins

IF YOU happen to find yourself driving to Rotherham from Barnsley, via the small town of Greasbrough, take care on the lonely winding road – particularly at night. Indeed, few of the narrow roads en route are illuminated by streetlights, so it is also a dangerous road for pedestrians. In fact, one pedestrian has been knocked down on this desolate road not once, it seems but several times . . .

Picture the scene. A dark, but clear night, in October 1980. A young man, whom I shall refer to as Mike Hanson, has just left his fiancee's house in the village of Nether Haugh (say 'Nether Hoff'), about two miles from Greasbrough. As this 18 year old negotiates his dusty, black car round the bend at the top of the hill, he begins his descent to the small town.

He knows the route along the Whins well; he has taken it many times in the past. The fields on either side of the road are open. A few hawthorn bushes dot the edges here and there but, even at night, Mike is treated to an otherwise uninterrupted and pleasant view of the surrounding area. As he passes a large house on the right, Wentworth East Lodge, of the Fitzwilliam Estate, he idly gazes at the property when – suddenly – something flashes in front of him, and he instinctively slams his foot on the brake.

An elderly lady has appeared from nowhere, and stepped right into the path of his car. A split-second before the car screeches to a halt, the short figure in a dark coat and hat, hits the front of the car and smashes into the windscreen. For an instant, the lady's shocked face is flung up against the window, as she stares in at the horrified

driver, then her body disappears over the roof, hurled at an awkward angle into the ditch to the left of the road.

Mike is in a daze. He sits a second or two to compose himself, his heart pounding against his chest. He's always been afraid of hitting someone – even though he wasn't speeding – and now it has finally happened. He twists the handle on the door, pushes it open and clambers out of the car, hurrying to the rear of the vehicle. Mike hopes upon hope that she is still alive, though he knows full well that a lady of that age, small and frail as she appeared, could not have survived the impact. He looks at the road beside the car, searching for the lady, almost apprehensively, for he knows that the sight which greets him will haunt him forever.

And it does. Though not in any way he could possibly have imagined.

The road is completely deserted. The tyres' skid marks are there. But all around is black and empty and deathly quiet. He remembers the ditch at the side of the road and hurries across. Still no one. He runs to the front of the car again. But there is no sign of her anywhere. Where is she?

Understandably, when Mike arrived home he was in an agitated state and very confused, to say the least. His mother tried to calm him down and suggested he phoned a friend of the family, Community Service Officer and former policeman of Rotherham Borough, Gordon Skelton.

I spoke to Mr Skelton who said he advised Mike to contact the police and report the matter to them as soon as possible, which he did, and he arranged for him and his mother to meet the police at the exact spot on the country road. The police spent considerable time and care checking the area at both sides of the Whins for the elusive victim, and they, too, drew a blank.

The police officer in charge shared Mike's confusion and asked for a description of the lady. Mike said that as far as he could remember, she was of small stature, wearing a coat and a bread-cob hat. The officer looked at him, then looked away, silent for a moment, before fixing him with a sober expression. 'Brace yourself, lad,' said the officer. 'What you saw was a ghost.' He went on to explain that Mike was not the only person to have seen the mysterious lady.

Mrs Hanson was still very sceptical, until the two passed the front of Mike's car and saw that the dust which he had previously noticed on the bonnet had been unsettled and partly wiped by something. So what was this? Physical evidence of a ghost which looked as solid and real as you or I? Perhaps. Certainly something had done it.

The reader may be wondering what, if anything, this has to do with a 'white lady'. Well, there is more to tell.

My research for this story originally began after an interview on BBC Radio Sheffield on the subject of the paranormal. The producers put a number of callers in touch with me. One was Graham Cheadle, whose experiences are documented in the chapter 'Who Ya Gonna Call?'; another was Mary Breedon, a former worker for the Probation Service, from Barnsley.

One night, in around 1985, Mrs Breedon was driving from Barnsley where she was due to attend a community service meeting at Masboro Street offices in Rotherham. As she passed through Nether Haugh, a figure in white rushed straight in front of her car! She slammed the brakes on, but the car hit the woman. She jumped out, to find no sign of the person.

Although Mrs Breedon did not report this to the police, she did tell one of the officers attending the same meeting that evening. That officer was Gordon Skelton, who subsequently told her of Mr Hanson's experience.

Two similar experiences on the same stretch of road with a five year gap. And some of the details seemed to tally. Mary Breedon was travelling downhill, and saw a figure rush from left to right, before it hit the car. Mike Hanson was travelling downhill and saw a figure rush from left to right, which also hit the car and was actually flung over the roof. However, while the Breedon and Hanson encounters seem to match in some ways, there is one major difference – the most significant detail, which we cannot afford to brush aside. Mary Breedon clearly remembers a tall lady dressed in white; Mike

Hanson was certain the figure he saw was a woman of small stature, in a dark coat and small hat. Indeed, Mrs Hanson, who related the story to me in her son's absence, explained that the details had been etched firmly in his mind, as he had experienced nightmares about the woman's face pressed against his car windscreen for a considerable time afterwards. So there were two extremely different descriptions of what I initially assumed was the same figure.

In addition, Mike Hanson's description is corroborated by the policeman who investigated the scene of the accident. According to him, a Rotherham bus driver, driving through Nether Haugh from Barnsley, actually watched the same figure rise up from the middle of the road in front of his bus! Although this caused him to swerve, luckily he avoided a crash and no one was hurt. Another witness had a similar experience, three months after Mike's encounter, not to mention other accounts of which the officer had vague recollection.

So – was Mary Breedon mistaken? Certainly she was the only person whose account did not tally with anybody else's. I contacted her again and asked, but Mary Breedon was quite sure she saw the tall lady in white.

The mystery deepened. In January 1999, as I neared the end of my research, I contacted two South Yorkshire newspapers, the *Rotherham Advertiser* and the *Rotherham Star*, who kindly printed articles recounting the two sightings, and my appeal for further information. Within a few days, I received a letter detailing an experience which stands out, in some ways, from both previous sightings, yet seems to corroborate Mary Breedon's encounter.

One early evening in 1980, 'Mrs Palmer' and her husband were driving down the Whins, from their home in Rawmarsh, to meet some friends. They, too, had just passed through the village of Nether Haugh, when she shouted to her husband to watch out for the figure which had appeared from the hedgerow at the side of the road.

The whole episode was over very quickly. When I spoke to Mrs Palmer, she was quite adamant about a number of points. Firstly, the car did not hit the figure. Secondly, the figure appeared from the hedgerow at the right of the road, rushing across their paths and disappearing through the corresponding hedgerow on the left – the opposite direction from the two previous sightings. Thirdly, she described the figure to me as a vague, transparent cloud, though with the noticeable outline of a woman. Mrs Palmer said that the lady unlike the one described by Mrs Breedon, was not particularly tall in height.

The final point, however, is by far the most intriguing. Her husband did *not* see the figure. He was not looking away from the road at that time; indeed, it would have been dangerous for him to do so on a road illuminated with nothing more than their car headlights. So if his wife saw it – why didn't he?

To make matters worse, as Mr Palmer had not seen the figure, he dismissed his wife's sighting as a figment of her imagination, as did the couple's friends when they arrived at their home. In fact, it was not until 1999 – nearly 20 years later – when she saw my article in the local paper, that Mrs Palmer realised what she saw all those years ago had been very real!

I was intrigued by Mrs Palmer's experience, and pleased too that I had inadvertently solved something which may have remained a mystery on her part for years to come – but it didn't bring me any nearer to solving the mystery. And there, unfortunately, I shall have to leave it. I have checked to see if there are any official records of the accidents, but all to no avail. If there used to be, then they have either been destroyed or relocated to another branch of the police. There is a vague tale of an old woman, travelling on a horse and cart, being killed at that spot – but this may be just a hand-down story which has been circulating the area for many years and have no basis in truth, or significance in this case.

Hopefully, someone who lives in another part of Yorkshire, or even further afield, who didn't see my appeal for information in the local press, will read this and perhaps throw new light on what, frustrating though it is, I am forced to label 'unsolved'.

15

The Haunting of Heath Farm

HEATH Farm is situated on the edge of the busy Dewsbury to Wakefield road – a more unlikely setting for a modern-day haunting would be difficult to imagine.

Built over a network of old mining tunnels, part of the farm is thought to date back to the 17th century. Once owned by the National Coal Board, until they forfeited ownership by losing the deeds to the land, it was sold to Mr Roger Sales.

Jackie and Graham Johnson took up residence in 1991, only after waiting two years for the price to drop in auction. However, when they moved in to Heath Farm they found that they had inherited something which was not mentioned in the sales brochure. Their attempts to find out more about the history of the property were largely unsuccessful.

Legend has it that the heath on which the farm stands has always had the reputation of being haunted. A single brick-lined tunnel leads from Heath Farm to the pub across the road which is thought to have been built on the site of the local gallows. The rugby club, three quarters of a mile away, stands in a direct line with the farm and the pub, and was exorcised in the early 1990s, after players and staff were troubled by the ghost of a young boy. Some local people have had eerie experiences there too. Children used to rush into the farm's properties as a 'dare', and a postman told of how he once saw a young boy in ancient dress, and surrounded by a strange glow, sitting at the side of the road crying.

The reasons behind Mr Sales' sudden departure have never been fully explained, but when the couple first visited the farm they found various odd things. The lightbulbs in one room suddenly exploded for no accountable reason, and they found salt sprinkled on the window sills, and in the corners, of the farmhouse, a devil's head doorknocker and a pentagram painted on the barn wall!

Also, there is a 'water problem' at Heath Farm. Animals can never be kept on the land, as the stables have constantly had to be rebuilt because of flooding. There seems to be a strange connection to water inside the farmhouse, too. One day, while Graham was running the bath, he went downstairs to chat to Jackie – and only a couple of minutes later water began to drop from the kitchen ceiling above them, which stands directly below the bathroom. Graham wondered how the bath could have filled up so quickly and overflowed, but he bounded up the stairs only to find the bath just half-full, with not the slightest sign of dampness. On inspection, the bath and pipes were totally undamaged, and the kitchen ceiling dried very quickly, leaving no water mark.

Jackie considers herself to be a natural psychic, but has never gone on to develop that talent because most of the messages she receives seem to be bad. However, through her 'gift', she has become convinced that there are many spirits evident at Heath Farm.

Jackie has seen a stocky lady with dark hair who appears in the farmyard, feeding chickens from her apron. She is thought to be responsible for switching the oven off when guests are expected for dinner!

Another spirit is that of an elderly man who sits in the corner of the workshop and disappears after a while. Workers from a local double glazing company downed tools and refused to work in the room when the old man kept appearing to watch them. The man is thought to be responsible for switching various machines and lights on and off and opening the workshop door at 3.30 pm every day without fail. However, Jackie and Graham say that they quickly got used to it, and are now no longer unnerved by his frequent appearances, disappearances and pranks.

The building which houses the farm offices seems to be haunted by an unseen entity who sends electrical machines haywire, including phones and faxes. Interestingly, this sounds like poltergeist activity, focused on a particular person. When Jackie is particularly stressed or wound-up she always takes a wide detour around the fax machine, because it starts printing out paper on its own.

The Johnsons had a visit from journalist Christine Wood, who was writing an article for the magazine of strange phenomena, *Fortean Times*, and she was shown around the farm's office building. At the time, Graham was frantically searching for a bunch of keys which he seemed to have mislaid. Christine had been idly staring at the front of the paper-shredding machine and, without moving away from the area, became aware that the keys were suddenly there. She was a little sceptical of it being caused by paranormal phenomena and wondered if it was a crude parlour trick, though pointing out that no one had been near the front of the machine in that time. Also, there was no evidence of trickery, no string or wire nearby and it was such a large cumbersome bunch of keys that the idea that someone had been playing a trick on her seemed very unlikely and virtually impossible. When Christine pointed out to Graham where the keys were, he made no attempt to suggest their reappearance had anything to do with the haunting. She had already been told that the main trick played in the office is hiding pens and keys, so Christine thought that perhaps the entity was simply trying to prove a point. Quite a mystery, thought Christine.

The main entity resident at Heath Farm appears to Jackie as much more sinister, and one which has a stronger influence. Often referred to as the Black Entity by her friend, professional medium Jeanette Ryan, it appears not to be the spirit of a human at all. Jackie calls it Beelzebub (pronounced Bee-elzi-bub). It is around 3'6" tall, is as hairy as a bear and has no human features, with a hunched back and 'piggy' legs. Jackie always knows when Beelzebub is around because there is a dirty, sweaty smell and when it touches her she gets an electric shock.

Her first sighting of this curious entity was while lying in bed one evening when Graham was away on business. Curiously, it appeared as a sort of dark shadow and could only be seen in any detail through the reflection in their wardrobe mirror.

It hung from the ceiling with an odd 'I know something you don't' expression on its face. Jackie was terrified and hid her head under the bedsheet, praying for it to go away, and it did after about 15 minutes.

Christine Wood asked if this could have been nothing more than a bizarre and vivid nightmare. Apparently not, as the entity has also been witnessed by Graham. This time they both saw it, again through the mirrored wardrobe, and it seemed to be jumping up and down outside their bedroom window, in a rather agitated fashion. When the couple reached the window and peered out they found it was being upset by one of their cats which they keep locked up in the stables at night.

The third sighting occurred one Christmas, when the couple had placed a novelty Christmas wreath on the front door, which played a familiar tune whenever anyone approached the house. One evening, Jackie heard the music and was confused when she peered out of the window to find no one near the house, and no cars in the drive. When the tune constantly replayed, she decided to go outside and investigate and saw Beelzebub darting back and forth in front of the sensor making the music play over and over again! By this time, Jackie wasn't frightened – just angry – and chased the entity across the farmyard, where it disappeared. She admits to feeling quite sorry for it, after that little episode.

Other odd happenings at Heath Farm are curious, to say the least, and remain a complete mystery. What Jackie and Graham term 'cloning' could possibly be better described as the appearance of 'ghosts of the living' or 'doppelgangers'.

Jackie once saw Graham appear in the kitchen then proceed to walk upstairs. After she called upstairs to tell him that dinner was ready, she found him in one of the offices at the other end of the building. There was only one staircase leading up to the upper floor, and the foot of the stairs had never been out of her sight for more than a few seconds.

One evening, Craig, an office worker at Heath Farm, called one of their dogs, Sassy. He watched her bounding across the field 500 yards away, and wondered if she could hear him. He was about to call again, but something made him look down to his side. Sassy was sitting there quite patiently. This happened on several occasions.

Phantom echoes are another phenomenon experienced by the workers. Oft-repeated phrases like 'call the dog' or 'call the horse' are often heard being thrown back across the yard after the person has just uttered them. Again, not particularly scary – just extremely puzzling.

On one occasion, the couple's manager Roger promised to tape a programme for them about a clergyman performing an exorcism in nearby Hull. On the couple's return from their night out, they ran the tape and heard a 'horrible voice' over the commentary which was talking about evil and the devil. As the actual exorcism ceremony on the programme was about to start, the tape switched itself off.

They asked Roger to take it home with him and test it on his own video recorder, which he did, and it worked perfectly.

Even in the early days, before they moved to the farm, Jeanette Ryan strongly advised the couple not to buy the property. Even now, she says that the best advice she can give them is to 'get the hell out of there'.

Jeanette visited the farm with Ken Mann, from the local newspaper, *The Dewsbury Reporter*, in early summer 1998, and had a strange experience while Ken was photographing her. On one of the photographs, Jeanette is holding a talisman designed to ward off evil spirits. However, both photos were partly blacked out by odd shapes. Mr Mann said that in his 25 years as a photographer he had never seen anything quite like it. He knew there was nothing to account for it as he peered through the viewfinder as the pictures were taken – no camera case, no fingers, nothing. He said he didn't believe in ghosts or anything of that nature – but could not find an explanation for the shapes on the photographs.

Jeanette has seen some of the spirits which Jackie has glimpsed – and a few more besides. There is a woman who cries for her child in the kitchen; a man called Ted who carries a shotgun protecting the farm; a group of children, all of them plague victims, who may be responsible for the strange goings-on in the office building; a man who hanged himself on the property; and the Black Entity, or Beelzebub, who is by far the strongest of them all.

Jackie believes that a lot of bad luck has befallen the couple because of the farm's phantom influences. Some of their pet dogs have died in mysterious circumstances, Graham's health has deteriorated while living there, and a number of business contracts have been lost to lower bids from companies which have since folded, though it would be unwise to say whether or not this has a direct bearing on the ghostly happenings!

Having said that, Jackie believes that the various entities don't mean them any real harm. However, the atmosphere in the house never lifts, and the only time Jackie and Graham feel better is when they leave the premises. What 'it' can do and what it creates does frighten her, and she added that they are both deeply unhappy, but have no choice for the moment but to live with it.

16

Ouija: Dabbling in the Dark Side

A NY tour of North Yorkshire would not be complete without a trip to Whitby – undoubtedly one of the most atmospheric towns you could ever hope to find. Its historic connections are numerous. The three ships which Captain James Cook took on his voyages of discovery in the Pacific – *Resolution, Discovery* and *Endeavour* – were all built in Whitby, and the local museum has a delightful display of artefacts relating to his connection with the town.

Sinister connections abound in Whitby, too. Devoted members of the Dracula and Vampyre societies congregate in the town for their annual get-together complete with fancy dress, much to the consternation of churchgoers and clergymen, some of whom view the festivities as a celebration of evil. For Whitby is the town which Bram Stoker selected for his character Count Dracula's entry into England, and the cemetery of St Mary's church was a real-life setting in the novel.

Accounts of ghosts and haunted houses, black dogs, hobgoblins and a variety of other fearsome apparitions all have their place in the folklore of Whitby. The most famous location is Whitby Abbey, said to be haunted by the ghost of St Hilda, who allegedly appears in a window of the ruins, overlooking the town.

However, not all the supernatural tales of Whitby are old legends. Modern phenomena are still reported from time to time, including the experiences of a resident whom I will call John Keith.

For several years now, John has lived in the 'new' part of Whitby, which is separated from the 'old' town by an iron swing bridge, spanning the River Esk. He has always been interested in the paranormal and so, during a rather long period of unemployment in 1994, he began to eke out a living by exploiting the mystical aspects of Whitby. He wrote and self-published a booklet on the ghosts and legends of Whitby, and sold it on a small market stall which he hired, along with various other occult-related wares such as astrology charts, runes, tarot cards and palmistry readings. The spare-time business quickly took off. By early 1995, he had become well-versed in such matters and was making house-calls with regular customers and arranging appointments for people to visit him.

It was about this time that he added another string to his bow and began making a ouija board. John does not believe himself to be psychically-gifted in any way, but he had heard that ouija worked for almost anyone who attempted to try it, so he thought it was worth a shot. He used an old round table which he had had for years, unscrewed the flat top and began work designing and painting the board. It took him about two weeks to complete the task, copying various prints of satanic pictures from library books onto the table-top. Meticulous in detail, John often worked into the night on the board until the project was finally finished.

John had enjoyed working on the table and if nothing came from it, he said he would not have viewed it as a waste of time. As it happens, the making of the ouija board did pay off – but certainly not in the way that he intended it to.

On the night he had completed the last bit of painting, John screwed the board back onto the table, and left old newspapers on the floor round the edges, just in case any paint dribbled onto the carpet. When he went downstairs into the lounge the next morning, all the newspapers had been crumpled up and left in a heap by the back door. He just could not work it out at all. Nothing else was out of place and there seemed to be no reason at all for this to have happened. That afternoon, his girlfriend Judith came to visit and brought her pet cat, Tigger. However, as soon as John opened the door, Tigger peered inside, snarling at something with her hackles risen up, and bounded off down the street. The couple went off to search for the cat but could not find her anywhere, much to Judith's distress. Tigger did return to Judith's flat one evening – though it was a full three days later. Where she had been, what she had been doing – and what had made her so frightened – remain a mystery to this day.

Some days, Judith would help John on the stall and then return to his house for lunch. When they did so one day in March 1995, a sudden tense atmosphere, which they later described as 'intensely claustrophobic', hit them head on as they entered the house. They both noticed and commented on it immediately and they became very wary and apprehensive of venturing further inside, so Judith suggested they buy a takeaway and return to her flat. John agreed, but said that he needed to pick up his wallet, which he had forgotten that morning. So he bounded up the stairs to his bedroom, grabbed the wallet from his bedside cabinet and started coming down again, when the hairs on the back of his neck just rose up.

John told me he would never forget that sensation. He just knew that someone was looking at him. He couldn't see or hear anyone, and there was no sign of a break-in so it couldn't have been an intruder, but he felt that someone was on the landing just a few feet away, staring down at him. For a few seconds he could hardly move, until Judith asked him what was wrong. John didn't want to scare her any more than she already was, so he just shook his head and returned to the door, and they immediately left the house.

At this point, John had not told Judith about the ouija board. He had kept a thick tablecloth over the design, deciding to keep it to himself for a while, which made him all the more surprised by Judith's next question. 'You haven't been using a ouija board, have you?' she asked. John was astounded. How had she known? She explained that as she was also interested in the supernatural she had experimented with ouija in the past and, although nothing physical happened, she had experienced similar sensations to the one they felt when they opened the door. John told her how he had converted the old table into a ouija board, and she implored him to take it from the house and burn it.

He promised he would but, although he had been unnerved by the sensations too, decided he was going to do no such thing, particularly because of all the hard work he had put into making it.

Having stayed the night at Judith's flat he returned the next day to find that the atmosphere had thankfully lifted. Although the feeling of being watched the previous evening had been so intense and was still fresh in his mind, he tried to put it down to imagination. Although why they should both share the same feeling at the same time, he could not fathom.

He made himself a cup of tea and some toast, then sat down on the sofa to work on an astrological chart and forecast a customer had ordered. About ten minutes into the work, he got the sudden feeling that someone was behind him. He was too scared to look round, as it felt as if the unseen thing was right behind him with its eyes burning into the back of his head. Summoning up all the courage he could muster, John leapt to his feet and, without turning round, shouted, 'Get the hell out of my house!' The feeling suddenly lifted and he felt that this was the end of it. But it wasn't.

That Sunday morning, he and Judith went to the local church service and, as they stood amongst the congregation praying, he noticed something very odd. The vicar who was holding the service kept casting sharp, angry looks straight at them – not to mention some of the more senior members of the congregation. John said that this was weird. It was almost as if they could sense that he had been using ouija, and that something had 'accompanied' them both into the church. At one point, Judith turned to him and in a whisper asked if he had kept his promise about burning the board. Slightly ashamed, John answered that he hadn't – but promised to paint over the symbols as soon as he got home that day. Judith said it would be better to burn it and rid himself of the thing – just in case.

With another icy stare from the vicar, John began to feel very uncomfortable, then nodded his agreement with Judith and sheepishly left the service early. Deciding that enough was enough, he went straight home, unscrewed the table-top ouija board, lit a fire in the back garden and burned it, until nothing remained but ash.

John Keith implored me to warn readers that they can never realise the effects using ouija can have on their lives, as he found to his cost. Since that day, nothing untoward has happened to Judith or him – and Tigger remains a regular visitor to the house!

17

Things That Go Bump in the Cell

THE former premises of the Calder Courts and police cells on Prescott Street, Halifax, have always been used for legal purposes, and the courts have been there since the 19th century. According to one source, mysterious goings-on have been experienced there for the last 60 years with a multitude of administrative and police personnel bearing witness to the phenomena.

Former policeman Alan Paley was stationed there in the mid-1970s. After being de-mobbed from the army, he worked at Skipton between 1948 and 1949, and then as a Relief Clerk in the West Riding Divisional Office for quite some time. Many odd things happened to him and his colleagues at the Courts building, and he sent me a list of around 20 people who could corroborate his statements.

There was a bell-board situated in the General Office (each bell was connected to a cell, for use by prisoners) and he recounted how it would activate of its own accord. Mr Paley points out that the bell-pulls would be pulled, thus activating the mechanism in the office, when the cells themselves were empty, and sometimes the whole of the cell area was unoccupied. They would go haywire, and yet a search of each cell would reveal nothing to account for the activity.

There was an old fashioned Victorian speaking-tube in the office which sent and received messages via the Magistrates' Clerks Office on the first floor. In each office there was a whistle connected to the tube; this was blown to let the other person know that you wanted to speak to them. Again, the whistle would sound at night – when there was simply no one present to operate it.

Mr Paley remembers mentioning the incident to his colleagues and *all* of them had had the same experience. At night time, the place was full of creaks and groans – typical of an old building. However, he points out that you could be sitting at a desk when a sudden, inexplicable chill would surge through the room and fill you with a strange, eerie feeling.

When my public appeal for information on the alleged haunting was published in the local press, including the West Yorkshire police paper, Mr Paley's was not the only reply I received. Another former constable, now a sergeant working in nearby Sowerby Bridge, remembers the night that he and a colleague were locking up the building, just before a shift ended. He entered the cell area on his own, and as soon as he had passed through the solid steel gate at the entrance, it slammed shut behind him! There was no draught and he could not see how it could have happened. Unable to budge the gate free, the constable shouted to his colleague, but to no avail. Eventually, with much effort, he had to climb up to a tiny window in one of the walls of the cell and squeeze his way out.

Indeed, this wasn't the only incident concerning the strange 'behaviour' of the cell block gate. When the Calder Courts and police cells were moved to new premises, a surveyor, Mr Jonathan Wilson, was appointed 'estate agent' and given the task of conducting tours around the building for prospective buyers. He was used to entering old and often decrepit buildings, as this was part of his job and it usually didn't bother him. But he says that walking through this particular building sent shivers down his spine.

Of course, the surveyor carried out his required duties to the best of his ability, but he told me he would try to get out as quickly as he could. There were two areas where he felt particularly uncomfortable: the toilets on the first floor and the cell area. Like countless others, he often felt an icy wind steal across the cell floor, and had also been overcome with a very real sense of dread, gloom and depression.

Returning to the mystery of the cell block gate, he told me he had all the keys to the building – and yet not one of them fitted the gate. Although it had no key, he had found it locked on occasion, and all efforts to prise it open proved unsuccessful.

One prospective buyer, a representative of the Halifax Christian Fellowship, was loaned the keys to the building in the surveyor's absence. When the man entered the building, the cell block gate was wide open but, before he left, having viewed the premises, he found it to be firmly shut and no amount of heaving and tugging could at first force it open.

At around the same time, the building was broken into by vandals and squatters and so a joiner was hired to board it all up, thus blocking possible entrances. Whilst working on the doorway – by then the only remaining entrance to the building – the joiner heard the distinct sound of footsteps in the corridor behind him, which ceased after a few seconds. Wondering what had caused the noise, he shrugged then continued with his work. On hearing the footsteps again, which sounded louder and closer, he decided to investigate, but could find nothing to account for the noises. However, on looking at the floor, he saw that some of the tiles in front of him had been broken, as if someone had been standing there, even though no one could have entered or left the building without passing him. Understandably terrified, the joiner completed the job as quickly as he could and left.

Mr Wilson pointed out that several people's experiences had tallied, often where the people involved had no knowledge of the building's haunted reputation, which suggests that over-active imaginations cannot be held solely responsible for the disturbances. As a practising Christian, Mr Wilson believes in the existence of evil spirits, and the influence they can have on people and places.

When the building was eventually sold, he hoped he would not have to visit the place again because, he said, there really is something very odd about it.

18

Secondhand Spook

JUNE and Peter Henderson have lived in the same terraced house in Doncaster for over ten years, since they moved from Royton, in Lancashire. They bought the property from the relatives of an elderly gentleman who lived there until his death in June 1990, and agree that the house itself has always had a very relaxed and welcoming atmosphere.

Five years passed at their address with nothing untoward happening – paranormal or otherwise – until one fateful day in March 1995. The couple went for a day out in Keighley and read somewhere that there was due to be an auction at a house clearance organised by a local estate agent. Always keen to spot a bargain, the couple arrived at the old house just outside the town centre and viewed the wares on offer. The one item which caught June's attention was an old cupboard measuring six feet high by three feet wide. She mentioned to her husband that it would provide much-needed storage space in the spare bedroom, which was now empty since their sons had moved away. When the auction started, there was little competition for the cupboard, and the couple secured it at a bargain price.

The estate agents kindly offered free delivery and the driver and his mate even carried it up the stairs for them when it arrived two days later. The Hendersons spent the next hour filling it up with some of the clutter from their own bedroom, and their task was soon completed. June mentioned that she had been unable to find one of her old dresses which she was sure she had kept and went to their bedroom to find it, while Peter stayed in the spare room.

Peter Henderson will remember that day for the rest of his life. Suddenly, the temperature dropped to freezing level. It was so sudden and without warning it made him gasp. It was not a warm day – but not particularly cold either. The windows were closed, and while there was always a slight draught from them, he could not attribute this sensation to that. The next thing he heard was the toilet flushing. Funny, he thought. He hadn't seen June go to the bathroom. She had gone to their bedroom on the right of the spare room, and he had not seen her walk past the door to reach the bathroom. He walked out of the room, onto the landing and pushed open the bathroom door. The toilet had indeed flushed, the bowl was filling up with water again, but June was not there.

Understandable then, that when June appeared behind him and touched his arm, he jumped a little. Peter asked if she had been to the bathroom, but she hadn't. Of course she hadn't. She couldn't have reached the bathroom, or left it, without him seeing her. Strange, too, that she hadn't heard the toilet flush either, although they could both hear the water pipes filling up again. He decided not to mention the cold spot by the cupboard, but just shook his head, mentioned that there must be something wrong with the plumbing, and simply left it at that.

About an hour later, as they were watching the TV in the living room, they both heard a single bump from upstairs. It wasn't a loud bang as if something had exploded, just a slight, but distinct thud which startled them a little, and they exchanged glances. Without saying a word, Peter got to his feet and went upstairs to take a look, with June close behind. What they saw astounded them. A small stool from the spare bedroom was lying on the floor of their own bedroom!

The couple just stood and looked on open-mouthed. They agreed that neither of them had taken the stool from the spare room and put it there. There was no reason they would have needed to do that anyway. The stool was always kept by the other side of the spare bed, between the bed and the window. June rarely moved it except for cleaning and she hadn't cleaned the room for quite a while. And even if they had moved it, how had it fallen over? It was a complete mystery. They returned the stool to its original position in the spare room, and went back downstairs.

For a week, nothing else happened. Neither of them went into the spare room as they had no reason to do so. The odd chill which they both noticed from time to time, always around the door of the room, and at the top of the stairs on the landing, did not strike them as strange enough to merit discussion. In fact, they only found out about their mutual experiences of the chill, when they experienced it together one day. It was exactly a week since they had bought the cupboard, when they revisited the room. June was the first in and what she saw stopped her dead in her tracks. She called to Peter and he rushed up the stairs to see what was wrong.

All of the clothes and shoes and other belongings which they had put carefully into the cupboard were strewn all over the bed. Their eyes went directly to where the stool should have been – but it wasn't and they found it wedged behind the door. The doors of the cupboard itself were closed – so even if by some ludicrous stretch of the imagination, a heavy traffic vibration or freak earth tremor had knocked all the belongings out of the cupboard, the doors would not have swung shut themselves. It was then that June and Peter told each other of the sudden icy chills they had both experienced over the last week. They decided not to move anything, leaving the clothes and the stool where they had found them, and hurriedly left the room, closing the door behind them. However, as they made their way back downstairs, a sudden chill hit Peter, which he later said felt as if someone had shot right through him. June experienced the same thing and the 'sensation' whooshed right past them as if it had sprinted upstairs.

Neither Peter or June had ever been very religious or spiritual or had the slightest interest or belief in the paranormal, but they could not find any other explanation for what they had experienced. Although the last thing they wanted to do was go telling everyone about it, they knew they needed help. A flick through the Yellow

Pages revealed a short list of spiritualist churches in the area and, even though the couple were apprehensive about contacting them, they decided to give it a try.

Following a telephone call to one of the numbers, they welcomed a visitor from the church, who called on them the very next morning. Medium Linda Russell explained that there was no need to be afraid. She assured the couple that there was no record of anyone ever having been harmed by a ghost. She said that dead people don't hurt you – it's only the living ones that do that.

Peter and June were about to tell Linda where they had felt the cold spots and suggest that the cupboard was at the root of the disturbances – but before they could say anything she made straight for the stairs and climbed to the top and halted. She asked the couple if she could go into the spare room, though neither of them had told her this was where the disturbances had occurred.

She motioned the couple to follow her in, and they stood there looking at their belongings in disarray on the bed. She closed her eyes for a minute and concentrated. After a while Linda said that the root of the trouble was an elderly lady who had owned the cupboard, and that while most spirits attach themselves to places, this lady had felt bound to the cupboard, since the house clearance had taken away most of her possessions after her demise.

The medium recited some prayers in the room, during which the chill returned for a moment, and then the atmosphere returned to normal. As Linda sat down with Peter and June over a cup of tea in the living room, she explained that most people don't become ghosts. Genuine hauntings, she said, are very rare. Perhaps only one out of a thousand people who die remain here for a reason: they have unfinished business; they are afraid to leave; or perhaps in a case of sudden death they are literally shocked out of their bodies and don't realise they're dead. Linda Russell concluded that people should not be afraid of ghosts, and the idea that they are to be feared and shunned was absolute nonsense. Death is just a natural part of life, she said.

As Linda was about to leave, June asked if it would be all right to keep the cupboard, since the atmosphere had lifted, and the medium said it would. But Peter had second thoughts. He persuaded June to donate it to a church charity sale, a week later. Just to be on the safe side!

19

Religious Wraiths at Bolton Abbey

FOUNDED in 1151, the ruins of Bolton Abbey (or Priory), stand amongst meadows, woods and waterfalls, and a more picturesque setting would be hard to imagine. Next to the 12th-century abbey is the parish church, with the nave last repaired and improved in 1864 and still used today, with a small footbridge and a row of stepping stones spanning the River Wharfe nearby.

As the scene has been one of peace and tranquillity for so long, it is not surprising that the shades of the past that haunt this particular spot are quiet and peaceful; unassuming wraiths which don't bother or frighten anyone.

An Augustinian canon has haunted the abbey ruins, church and rectory for hundreds of years. The latter stands on what is believed to be the original site of the former priory gatehouse, and the canon was often seen by the owners. The Reverend James MacNab, while serving as the rector of Bolton Abbey just prior to the First World War, was asked for a written account of his experience by none other than King George V. Like other monarchs, such as Queen Victoria, King George took a keen interest in spiritualism and the unseen world and, having heard secondhand tales of encounters with the canon, he requested further information.

Rev MacNab related experiences witnessed by many over the years, including himself and his family, and the Marquis of Hartington who was visiting at the time. Hartington had seen a figure standing by the doorway to his bedroom. It looked like a monk dressed in a long ankle-length garment like a dark-coloured dressing-gown, either black or brown, with a greyish hood. The figure looked quite real, and the Marquis saw him at extremely close quarters. A bright-eyed elderly man, around 65 years of age, of average height and with a week's growth of stubble on his chin, with a round and happy wrinkled face. Hartington was astonished and rushed downstairs to call the Rector – but when the two returned to the landing, the monk had gone. The Marquis said that there was no question of the ghost being transparent in appearance, but just as solid as any actual man.

Others saw him – or another figure – and dubbed him 'the spectral black canon', who wore a black cassock-like robe, black cloak and, in this case, a flat, black hat.

From the mid-1920s to the present day, more people reported seeing him including Lord Charles Cavendish, and also a woman who recounted childhood experiences with this friendly spirit, whom she and her friends called 'Punch', due to the pointed hood which she said the canon always wore. He is still seen today and is often glimpsed by visitors, usually in the summer months, walking towards the gatehouse.

In the 1970s, the then rector, the Reverend Frederick Griffith Griffiths, recounted the various sightings witnessed by himself and his family. The clergyman said they had seen the canon so many times that they fully accepted him as part of the building – and even a member of the family. They could also sense his presence without actually seeing him, and there was often the aroma of incense and fermenting mead floating through their home!

His first experience, which was so vivid it remained fresh in his memory for years to come, occurred one morning while he was shaving in the bathroom. On glancing through the window, he saw a figure standing in the grounds of the priory. Thinking it was a summer visitor having a look round that early summer's morning, he went down to meet the man and found, on closer inspection, that the figure was dressed as a black canon. It was then that he realised he was watching a ghost. It was almost a year later that the Rev Griffiths saw him a second time, walking towards the priory church.

After that, he encountered the monk on many occasions. One afternoon, he was busy sawing timber in the cellar, when he heard the curious slapping of sandalled feet along the floor above, even though he was alone in the house at the time.

His daughter Lynn had seen the monk many times walking alongside the flesh-and-blood congregation, accompanying them as they made their way along the church path – but when questioned later about the phantom's appearance they swore they had seen no one!

He is most often seen within the priory ruins and especially in the Old Choir section of the church. Groups of people have seen him walking peacefully through the ruins and have often heard organ music emanating from the otherwise empty church, with the organ power-room locked and the only key in the rector's pocket! It is also on record that countless visitors, including a former Archbishop of York, have heard the 'angelus' ringing at Bolton Abbey, even though the bells have long been removed.

Because of the differing descriptions of the canon, it could be that there are several religious wraiths haunting the Abbey grounds; perhaps a few members of the Augustinian religious order, disinclined to leave and thus clinging to the immediate vicinity. The former rector's wife, Mrs Mary Griffiths, said she was convinced there was a variety of different forms, though all with a religious background. Her belief is based on one particular experience where she watched two of what she calls 'the Holy Fathers' cross the room in which she was sitting. They walked right past her, with no acknowledgement and just 'dissolved' in the solid stone wall, which is seven feet thick in that part of the rectory.

The most dramatic sighting occurred in the late 1970s when a lorry driver, who was delivering coal to the rectory, slammed on his brakes and screeched to a halt in the small lane which runs past the driveway. Thinking there had been an accident, the Rector rushed out to see the driver peering under the wheels of his truck, with a confused and dazed expression. The driver explained that he had quite clearly seen the figure of a monk in his headlights and, although he tried to stop, was convinced he had unavoidably hit the man. Needless to say they couldn't find a body to account for the episode – and the driver was more than a little sceptical when told of the resident spooks!

It is not only during the summer months that odd figures are seen flitting through the ruins of the Abbey. In February 1993, Stephen and Edith Ash, of Greater Manchester, stopped off at Bolton Abbey one cold, but bright and sunny afternoon while touring North Yorkshire villages. Edith spotted a tall figure in a black robe and hood at the rear of the church, and called her husband over to tell him. While they were not surprised to see a man in a habit in such a religious setting, the black colour certainly occurred to them as rather odd. Their Yorkshire terrier Cindy started barking when the figure vanished at the rear of the church, and nearly broke her collar, until Edith let her go and watched her bound off after the man. When the couple reached the spot there was no sign of anyone, but Cindy was rooted to the spot for quite some time, staring and barking at the back of the church wall.

Subsequent enquiries failed to reveal who the man may have been, though it would be interesting to know if there used to be a door at the back of the church. If it was a ghost, then perhaps he had disappeared through what was once a doorway, which has since been bricked up. The behaviour of the dog was curious, too. Most ghostly presences have the opposite effect on animals in that they refuse to go anywhere near the area – perhaps religious wraiths possess a welcoming disposition and draw visitors to them rather than filling their hearts with fear and dread. However, one thing is for sure – the ghosts of Bolton Abbey have been there for hundreds of years and may remain there for hundreds more – a fruitful site for ghost-hunters!

20

Licensed to Serve Spirits

GREAT Britain has been known for centuries as the Haunted Isle or 'isle of spirits', and there are said to be more ghosts here per square mile than in any other country in the world. So, then, what type of location in this haunted isle most regularly features in reports of ghostly goings-on? Castles, halls, theatres, stately homes? No. Pubs.

Since time immemorial, public houses, or inns, or taverns, have been considered to be – like churches – the centre of the community in small villages and bustling towns and cities alike. Places where people could spend their leisure hours talking, laughing, relaxing, and enjoying themselves. But inns have also borne witness to the harsher sides of life. Fights break out in pubs, tempers flare – and people die: in scuffles, in fights, in arguments. People, too, tend to pass away in the most relaxed of atmospheres; over a pint in their favourite chair by the roaring log fire. Indeed, landlords themselves may spend their final days here, not quite knowing when 'Time' will ultimately be called.

Skeldergate in York is a favourite corner of the city, and boasts a colourful and famous history. Fairfax Street and Buckingham Street, in particular, are connected to one of the most famous haunted taverns in Britain, the Cock and Bottle Inn.

It was built on the site of a house belonging to George Villiers, the second Duke of Buckingham, a devout Royalist supporter during the Civil War but viewed by many as something of a dark horse. Villiers was born in 1627 and, after much extensive travelling, settled in

England at the onset of the Civil War. He fought alongside the Royalist forces in the battles of Nonsuch and Worcester. Defeated, he fled England after being outlawed, but later returned, though in fear of his life, and married Mary, the daughter of Lord Fairfax. In his *History of York*, Francis Drake recounts that during the Duke's residence at the timbered house on Skeldergate, Villiers built a laboratory. His main passion was alchemy and he spent much of his fortune on the attempt to transmute base metals into gold. Some critics also fired accusations at him for practising Black Magic and Satanism in his desperate quest for wealth and power. Soon after returning to England, he was imprisoned in the Tower of London, and later Windsor Castle, by Cromwell for his part in the Civil War, but after the Restoration, returned to his home and became a very close acquaintance of Charles II. His loyalty was rewarded with various titles including Lord Lieutenant of the County of York – and he proceeded to encourage the monarch in all manner of folly and vice.

Villiers' house was later turned into a pub, The Plumber's Arms, which was pulled down by Smith's Brewery Company in 1962, to be replaced by a more modern building. This building, which became the Cock and Bottle, inherited some of the original 16th-century timbers and panels from Villiers' home – and it is this which lends credence to the theory that Villiers is the ghostly resident seen and sensed by numerous people over the years.

When licensees Peter and Brenda Stanley moved into the premises in November 1973 neither believed the story of the ghost. All previous details had been vague and unsubstantiated over the years – until Mrs Stanley saw it. She was sitting in the lounge upstairs watching TV when she turned to see the figure of a man standing behind her. He did not appear to be solid (as ghosts usually and surprisingly seem to be reported) but she was able to note quite a few alarming details. She could see his head and shoulders and long, black wavy hair, a lump on the end of his chin, a big nose and one eye visibly bigger than the other. Once she realised she wasn't looking at a real flesh-and-blood person, she became extremely

107

frightened – at which the man merely smirked and vanished through the wall!

Mrs Stanley had no idea who the ghost was until a friend showed her portraits of famous historical figures. She picked out the face immediately: the ghost matched the portrait of Villiers exactly. Since her first sightings, Mrs Stanely has often felt him looking at her as she lies in bed at night and sometimes, while at the bar has felt a sudden cold sensation on her shoulders and arms, 'like a deep-freeze cold', which has been reported by bar staff and customers alike. This feeling often passes from person to person as they sit together chatting at the bar. She also hears him moving about and murmuring. Electronic apparatus placed on the bar, like tape recorders, have failed to work for some unknown reason.

A whole host of other phenomena have been reported by successive licensees, bar staff, cleaners and customers alike. The bar lights suddenly dim for no apparent reason even though the electricity supply is in working order and the other lights in the building remain unaffected. A heavy door, with a strong spring, has been seen and heard to open without human agency, and other doors lock and unlock themselves without the use of a key. Pictures regularly fall off walls in the Cock and Bottle and small objects mysteriously vanish only to turn up at a later date in the most curious of places. The most striking of the phenomena though has been the appearance of a figure in a wide-brimmed hat sitting at one of the tables in the pub – there one minute and gone the next.

Another landlord told of his family's encounters with a poltergeist which would hurl things around the bar. His stepfather was also one of the family to be unaccountably rooted to the spot in an upstairs corridor, held by an unseen force and temporarily rendered unable to move.

However, possibly the most alarming aspect of the paranormal activity is the dislike of the crucifix which one landlord's mother used to wear as a pendant. Some unseen hand would pull it off and throw it to the floor and when her sceptical son jeered at her story and wore it round his wrist the same thing happened to him.

Successive landlords have since forbidden the wearing of crucifixes on the premises because it seemed an obvious and pointless way of attracting trouble!

The skeleton of an unknown person was found by archaeological students excavating the site of Buckingham's house, at the point where his library once stood. Is the ghost that of this person or is it, as Mrs Stanley surmises, the restless spirit of the Duke himself? The mystery continues. . .

Following an interview on Radio Leeds, I received a letter from Mrs Elaine Armer who, with her husband and daughter, took over the premises of the White Cross Inn, Bradley, Huddersfield in 1988.

The first alarming thing they experienced was the sound of footsteps, which they would hear from their bedroom last thing at night. The steps would come from the direction of the large function room, down a passageway, through to their living quarters, and past their bedroom. The footsteps always seemed to head straight for the bathroom, then, bizarrely, Mrs Armer would hear the lavatory flush soon afterwards. On the few occasions she climbed out of bed to see who was making the sounds, she could always see the toilet bowl refilling as it does after being flushed. Strangely enough, her husband and daughter were always sound asleep when this occurred, though Mrs Armer was certainly not the only person to have an odd experience at the White Cross.

The next thing that happened was the continual appearance of puddles of water all over the floors where no water had been. One night, their daughter's bed was found soaking wet and she was unable to use it for the next four nights while it was drying out.

Whatever the truth behind their uninvited guest, it seemed very fond of turning on the gasses of the lager pumps in the cellar, and every morning the couple would find that about two pints of mild had been pulled and was in a puddle on the floor behind the bar. The couple called in the brewery and a plumber but both inspections drew a blank. There seemed nothing to account for it.

One night, just after closing time, Mrs Armer's husband told her not to turn off the lights in the gents' toilets, as he had just seen someone go in. Needless to say, when he checked the toilets they were completely empty. Although Mrs Armer never actually saw the ghost, a few other people did including her husband, and they soon agreed that it was a former landlord.

Mr Steve Roberts (a pseudonym) was a landlord at the White Cross Inn some time ago and had died on the premises, while in his mid-sixties. Mr Armer and a couple of the regulars who had actually seen the ghost were particularly unnerved because they had known Mr Roberts when he was alive. In fact, one of the customers was terrified and flatly refused to go to the toilets on his own again. In addition, one of Mrs Armer's friends, Sue, had seen the man. She had been looking in a mirror at the inn one evening, joking with her friend with the rhyme 'Mirror, mirror, on the wall, who is the fairest one of all?' when the figure of a man appeared in the reflection behind her, though when she turned and looked, he was nowhere to be seen.

Eventually, the couple thought that enough was enough and called in Mrs Armer's friend who is a medium. She had helped the licensees of the Three Nuns Inn, at Mirfield, rid their pub of a ghostly influence some time ago and she visited the White Cross Inn with an open mind. She attempted to channel her psychic gift to contact the spirit they had all come to know as Steve, though she told me that there was evidence of other spirits living within the confines of the building as well. She explained to me that Steve had become earthbound after his death, intent on searching for his wife who, by that time, had long since left the pub and was resident in a nursing home. The medium, who prefers not to be named, lit a candle in each room, said a prayer and, eventually, the atmosphere returned to normal. Nothing else was experienced there again. In addition, Mr and Mrs Armer discovered that Mr Roberts' favourite tipple was mild which would seem to explain why two pints of that particular beer had been pulled from the pumps each morning, and left in a pool on the floor.

Though why anyone – including a ghost – would waste good beer, is a complete mystery!

21

Ghosts Galore at Treasurer's House

THE ancient city of York boasts two record-breaking titles with a ghostly nature. Widely considered by many to be 'the most haunted city in Europe', beating London and Bath as contenders for possessing more ghosts per square mile than anywhere else, York also contains Treasurer's House, on Chapterhouse Street, which is listed in the *Guinness Book of Records* for housing the oldest ghosts on record.

The Roman centurions of Treasurer's House have spurred many a television documentary, as have the other ghosts which allegedly walk the building. One such documentary was made by a Dutch TV company who hired two 'witches', or mediums, to visit the premises to see if they could pick up any psychic vibrations from the past. One of them contacted the presence of a man who was being held in an ecclesiastical prison nearby. He said there was a fire sweeping through the city and was in great fear of his life as no one had come to free him, and he is thought to have perished in the fire.

The fire sounded like the one that ripped through York in 1856 and, while the 'witches' could easily have read literature about this historical tragedy, they would probably have been unaware that one such ecclesiastical prison had been situated near to Treasurer's House. This was only discovered by the Administrator after much study of reference documents at the library.

Among the other presences is George Aislaby who was carried to the building, having been mortally wounded in a duel. Some visitors have felt 'an acute sense of needing to protect themselves from some violent attack', when passing the door in Chapterhouse Street, a sensation attributed to Aislaby's presence. This antagonistic atmosphere has also been sensed in the vicinity of the door leading to the garden overlooking the same street.

In the north-east corner of the building, the Tapestry Room dates from the 17th century and is lined with blackened wooden panels from that period. For some reason, this part of Treasurer's House is by far the coldest area of the building and remains so, even during the summer months. Here, there is the vague tale of a wife who murdered her husband when he took on a mistress – though admittedly there is little historical detail to verify this account.

There can be few serious students of the subject, however, who have not heard of the Roman soldiers seen by Harry Martindale, in the ancient cellars during the early 1950s. This became a classic case in the history of psychic phenomena because, although there had been other witnesses to the phenomenon, Harry was the only one to offer public testimony in recounting his experience, and his descriptions of little-known historical details astounded experts on Roman history.

It was around 1953 when Harry Martindale, then an apprentice plumber, found himself working in the cellars at Treasurer's. His small ladder was propped up against the wall, where he busied himself with the task of installing central heating pipes to the cellar roof. Ghosts were certainly the last thing on the young man's mind. The installation had commenced the previous day – which had passed wholly without incident.

It began with a single sound in the distance, although he could not say from which direction it came. It reminded him of a military bugle being blown, though he shook his head and dismissed it as that of a car horn echoing from the street above. Suddenly, he saw an object emerge from the wall his ladder was leaning against, and he jumped to the floor in shock. As Harry hit the ground then scrambled to the far corner of the cellar to escape whatever it was, he found what appeared to be the figure of a man in Roman dress emerging through the solid stone wall.

Dumbfounded, he watched as the man was followed by between 12 and 20 soldiers, one riding a horse, who marched through the stone wall and dissolved into the opposite side of the cellar. The young Harry was understandably terrified and considered making for the exit, but the procession was barring his way. He would just have to sit tight and wait for the vision to end. He was amazed – and relieved – that the Romans did not turn to him. The room in which he had been working in the cellar was such a small, enclosed space – and the proximity between the advancing soldiers and him was so close, that he expected them to turn and confront him – but they didn't. They just continued on their course, stumbling along, looking very tired and dispirited, with their uniforms splattered in mud.

The most amazing thing that Harry remembers about the soldiers is that they appeared to be cut off at the ankles. At that time, archaeological excavations had been made in the cellar and it was only when the soldiers reached the dip where the work had been carried out (which turned out to be the original level of the floor raised in the intervening years) that their full figures came into view.

The vision was not without sound. Harry heard a sort of low murmuring, presumably from the soldiers, sounds from the horse as it clopped along the ground, and a sort of 'muffled tread' as the figures of the men followed on in suit. The last sound he remembered was another bugle call from a short, straight horn, which he actually saw the last soldier press to his lips and blow, as the latter disappeared with his comrade through the opposite wall. As the sound of the horn died away into the distance, the young plumber scrambled to his feet and made for the exit. Still in a state of shock, he desperately staggered through labyrinthine tunnels of the cellar until he reached the flight of steps and hurried up, coming face to face with the curator. The elderly man took one look at him and said: 'You've seen the Romans, haven't you?'

A great sense of relief flooded through him, as Harry realised he was not going mad after all; that others had witnessed the same amazing spectacle. Some had even entered details in a book which the curator showed to him, and he was encouraged to enter his own recollection while the experience was still fresh in his mind.

Harry wrote that the soldiers' appearance had not been what he would have expected had he ever dreamt of meeting a Roman centurion. Like most people, the only Romans he had ever seen were actors in Hollywood epics; big, strapping men with shiny, well-polished uniforms marching proudly through the streets. And yet the sight which had confronted him was exactly the opposite. The first soldier he saw was of a considerably short stature, looking very weary and haggard. He wore leather sandals thonged to the knee; a kilt unevenly dyed in green and made of a rough, sack-like material; and a helmet ordained with a colourful plume of birds' feathers. He was carrying a short sword, hanging in a scabbard. In addition, the sword was hung at the soldier's right side, rather than the left. This was another minute detail, not widely known, which convinced the historians that Harry's experience was wholly authentic.

The previous witnesses of the phantom legion all preferred to remain anonymous, though their descriptions did tally with Harry's experience. One of them was an American gentleman who had read somewhere that the Roman legion was said to appear on a particular night, once every seven years. This seems far too long for any self-respecting ghost-hunter to wait, but the idea apparently paid off! The man lay in wait for them, and then watched them appear and file through the cellar as expected. Sadly, the book containing all the testimonies has been mysteriously spirited away.

However, another entry noted in the book involved a lady who was a guest at a Treasurer's House fancy dress ball, which had been thrown by the last owner on the eve of handing over the ownership to the National Trust. Walking down a passageway, she encountered a man in Roman costume. On approaching him, the lady was quite upset when he sternly barred her way with his spear. When she complained to the host of the man's rude behaviour, demanding to know the name of the guest, she discovered that there was no one answering the man's description at the party, and a subsequent search of the house revealed nothing.

114

A particularly interesting account comes from the wife of a former caretaker of the House, who was in the habit of entering the cellars to get some coke for the solid fuel stove upstairs.

On one such occasion, the couple's pet dog, who would normally accompany her on this errand, refused to budge past the top of the cellar steps and stood there whimpering. As the lady walked along the first long passage, she heard someone following her. Suddenly petrified, she turned round, to see four or five horses being led along the passage by Roman soldiers, rapidly approaching her – but on a second look they had gone. As in Harry's case, these soldiers did not acknowledge her or seem to be aware of her presence, and both soldiers and horses actually seemed to be cut off at the knees, as if they were again standing on the original level of the ground. In her time at Treasurer's House, this lady had two further encounters, but had been unaware of any previous reports.

Around November 1975, psychical researcher and author Steve Cliffe assembled a small group of investigators to research the phenomena and was granted permission from the National Trust to set up cameras and other electronic equipment in the haunted cellars. The group were hoping for some success at this time of year, as much of the activity is reported during the winter months. When they arrived the following morning to retrieve the equipment they found that various sounds had been recorded.

Heavy footsteps and car horns were quickly dismissed, attributed to pedestrians and drivers on the street above, but many of the findings seemed beyond explanation.

The sounds of metallic 'chinks' were recorded which remain a mystery to this day, not to mention the sound of someone moving around near the microphone – the curator had instructed the staff to keep out of the cellars during the duration of the investigation, and they often remained locked and unvisited for several days at a time. Also recorded, was the sound of someone breathing very heavily, perhaps forcibly, near the microphone. Of particular interest to the group, due to the known nature of the haunting, was the odd sound of leather sandals flopping on a flat surface, as such a surface was not in existence in the vicinity of the equipment, consisting as it did of rubble due to the ongoing excavation work. Intriguing, too, was the occasional steady, rhythmic sound of someone beating a kettle-drum. While Steve Cliffe tried to recreate the sound by banging a dustbin lid from the street above, his companions found the clatter did not match the drum-beat, which, at any rate, was barely audible.

The investigations continued until February and among the most interesting sounds, which seemed to tie in with the Martindale encounter, was a single blast on something which sounded like a foghorn. Possible explanations such as sounds from York train station were suggested but quickly ruled out: the station is a considerable distance from Treasurer's House, and the sounds, too, are quite dissimilar.

So what was it? Could it have been the lone bugle call from one of the Roman soldiers marching through the cellar?

Many years after the experience, which remains firmly etched in his memory, Harry posed this question about the Romans: 'Do they come once, or twice, or three times a day, whether there is anyone to see them or not?'

Now, there *is* a question. Do ghosts appear automatically, at certain times, like clockwork? Do the dead seek acknowledgement from the living? Do they need to be observed in order to appear?

The important evidence of the tape recordings collected by Steve Cliffe and his dedicated group certainly suggests not.

22

Temple Newsam: The Most Haunted House in Yorkshire?

Having read somewhere that Chingle Hall, near Preston, is often dubbed 'the most haunted house in Lancashire', I wondered if I would find a Yorkshire equivalent in my research. I didn't have to look far.

Temple Newsam is a large Jacobean mansion situated five miles to the east of Leeds, and stands in a huge park which boasts many historic connections. As the birthplace of Lord Darnley, consort to Mary, Queen of Scots, it was the centre of much political intrigue. Originally owned by the Knights Templar, in the 12th century, the house came into royal ownership when their activities were finally suppressed after accusations of witchcraft and heresy. The estate was passed on to the D'Arcy family, and then in 1537, Sir Arthur Ingram took over the ownership. He made various architectural additions as did subsequent owners towards the end of the 18th and 19th centuries.

Frequently described as 'the Hampton Court of the North', because it was constructed mainly of warm red brick, I discovered that there are other similarities with London's royal residence. Not only is it packed from wall to wall with fine collections of portraits, ceramics, silver and furniture, but its ghosts are numerous, too.

Before Temple Newsam passed into public ownership, when Lord Halifax sold it to Leeds Corporation (now Leeds City Council) in 1922, he had the good fortune to see the most well known of the ghosts. He recorded his experience in his famous *Ghost Book*.

Lord Halifax's account told of how he had awoken at four one summer's morning in 1908, to watch an elderly lady of great beauty dressed in a blue frock and lace shawl, glide across the bedroom. She paused at the dressing table, apparently searching for something and then left via the Miss Ingram Room, adjoining it. Lord Halifax immediately lit a candle and followed her, but she was nowhere to be seen. The ghost has now come to be known as the Blue Lady, and the bedroom is named in her honour, the Blue Damask Room, or simply the Blue Room.

A room in the North Wing, where Lord Darnley is said to have been born, is haunted by two ghosts: a young boy who steps out of a cupboard and wanders around restlessly, and one of the original Knights Templar who prowls around the room and nearby corridors with a foul look on his face!

The South Wing of Temple Newsam, though, seems to possess much of the paranormal phenomena which, by all accounts, is still active to this day. Visitors and staff, while in the Red Room, have heard spine-chilling screams of agony coming from nowhere. The door of an old bedroom, known simply as Room No 4, is often seen to slowly open and close without human contact, and occupants have heard the sound of sighing when there is no one else present. A particularly curious occurrence reported by users of this room is the sound of heavy furniture being dragged across the boards on the floor below, even though people who have been present downstairs have never heard a thing. It has been suggested that these sounds are echoes of yesteryear when dances used to be regularly held, and the furniture moved to the edge of the room to accommodate the guests. This particular haunting is, therefore, often referred to as the Phantom Ball.

The most frequently seen ghost, and long-time spectral resident, must be the monk-like figure in a brown habit which has been witnessed by people across the centuries in the Long Gallery. In the early 1970s, a visiting couple from Huddersfield watched the figure emerge from the gallery, enter the chapel, walk across to the organ and vanish. They described it as 'a most malevolent-looking creature'!

During the Second World War, a foreman working at Temple Newsam had a brief glimpse of this apparition while doing his rounds one night near the chapel. Punching the time-clocks as he went, Mr William Vickers popped his head round the door of a side room near the chapel to see what he described as 'a misty, flimsy outline' appear in the facing doorway at the far end. He looked away for a moment but on turning back it had vanished. A second or two later, he had done the same! Finding his way to the ground floor, his companion, Mr Bill Waring remarked: 'You look as if you have seen a ghost!'

I must thank the member of Leeds City Council who sent me an article which featured in the December 1949 issue of the periodical, *Yorkshire Illustrated.* Although it is greatly outdated, I refer to it here because its writer, Grace Gladwin, succeeded in throwing new light on the mysterious Blue Lady, and offered accounts of two hitherto unrecorded hauntings.

Ms Gladwin recounts how she was shown a manuscript by a Mr William Earnshaw of Leeds, who inherited it from an ancestor of his, Mr James Earnshaw. According to the author the book, written in 1751, was not merely intended as a catalogue of the folklore and legends of Temple Newsam, but an earnest endeavour to find the true facts concerning the origins of these ghost stories.

The Blue Lady is supposed to be a relative of the Ingram family who resided at Temple Newsam in the reign of Charles II. Unfortunately, she received quite a shock in her early years which seems to have left its mark upon her for the rest of her life. While travelling home from visiting her friends one day, her coach was attacked by three robbers who threatened her and stole everything of value. Following this, she became obsessed with hoarding her possessions and was known to have devised hiding places in which to keep her valuables.

Many witnesses of Miss Ingram's ghost have noticed the distinctive scar above her right eye which, although absent from her portrait which hangs on a wall of the house, is thought to have been a physical wound inflicted by the robbers. In 1926, a gentleman visitor gave a detailed description of a woman dressed in Carolean garments with a scar above her right eye. He had seen her standing in a doorway, although he had known nothing of the story of the Blue Lady beforehand.

Another tale which falls in with the factual history of the house concerns the ghost of the White Lady. When the book was written, the house was the residence of the Viscount Irwin who related the account to the author: Lady Jane Dudley, a ward of the Countess of Lennox, was so in love with Lord Darnley that when she heard of his betrothal to Mary, Queen of Scots, she fled to her room and hanged herself with her girdle. The apparition is said to haunt the part of the building which was added in the 16th century, the structure of which has been altered over the years.

In 1735, a serving maid went into convulsions after encountering the White Lady, who she later said was dressed in a white robe, a lace cap and a small ruff. It took quite some time for the maid to recover from her experience. Over one and a half centuries later the apparition was still being seen when, in 1891, a maid who had been employed by the family for many years gave an identical description of Lady Jane.

A murder took place at Temple Newsam in the early 18th century, and it was detailed in a rare pamphlet described as 'The last dying speech of William Collinson, a manservant at Temple Newsam, Yorkshire seat of Viscount Irwin, who was hanged for the murder of Phoebe Gray, a maid servant at Temple Newsam.'

The story is that in 1704, a large bonfire was lit in the grounds of Temple Newsam to celebrate the victory of Marlborough at the Battle of Blenheim, and all the family, servants and folk from neighbouring estates were invited to attend the event. While the people were gathered outside, heartily eating and drinking, manservant William Collinson sneaked up to see Phoebe whom he was very much in love with. Just exactly what was discussed has never been determined but it resulted in Collinson strangling the girl and disposing of her body down a well in the house. Eventually, she was found, and when a fellow servant testified to having seen Collinson in the vicinity of her room, on the night of her disappearance, he was arrested. A confession of his guilt was obtained and he was duly hanged at York.

Collinson's ghost had been witnessed many times in the 18th and 19th centuries, and at least two sightings have been reported in the 20th century. An elderly maid employed at the hall in the 1930s told how she had seen what she described as a serving man in a very old costume, which matched exactly the description of a manservant in the time of Lord Irwin's residence. A near-identical report was recorded by a Mrs Dare, whose husband was in charge of the hall at that time. Visitors who have slept in the room next door to Phoebe Gray's room have often been awoken by a curious tapping noise, as though the heels of a woman's shoes were being dragged along the floorboards.

With the sightings of so many ghosts – ancient and modern – it could just be that Temple Newsam is the most haunted house in Yorkshire. Indeed, perhaps it is the only serious contender of Chingle Hall, for the title of 'the most haunted house in England'?

Shadows at My Side

WHEN the county of Humberside was born in April 1974, Yorkshire lost more than just the East Riding. Ghosts and legends galore dot the county from side to side, which include many of the more well-documented of British hauntings.

The famous poltergeist of Wesley's home, Epworth Rectory, is still hailed as a classic case to this day; the screaming skull of Anne Griffith reputedly continues to cause anxiety to the visitors of Burton Agnes Hall; and the lovely village of Beverley still competes with Pluckley (Kent), Bramshott (Hampshire) and 'chilling' Chipping (Lancashire) as one of the most haunted villages in England.

The Inland Revenue office built on the site of the old Tivoli theatre in Hull boasts the ghost of Arthur Lucan (aka Old Mother Riley), where the entertainer died; and the multitude of pubs, theatres and private homes with non-paying tenants only add to that number.

It is a sobering thought, though, that despite the many reputedly haunted sites in the county, which would leave any self-respecting tour operator foaming at the mouth, one Hull man claims to have been visited by even more apparitions within the four walls of his own house.

There is an old saying that if you are born the seventh son of a seventh son then you will be gifted with 'second sight', now commonly referred to as ESP. While this is not an exclusive right to 'the gift' (and sexist in the extreme!), it does make a point: that naturally psychic people are few and far between.

Bill Adamson remembers the first – and last – time he attended a spiritualists' meeting. He had popped in one evening, merely out of curiosity, and was almost immediately singled out by the Healer who was talking to them. Bill recalls being quite unnerved when the Healer stopped speaking, looked directly at him, and approached. With a whisper he asked if Bill would stay behind after the meeting for a chat as it was obvious he had the ability to train as a medium. Utterly bewildered, Bill did stay behind and the Healer told him he saw an aura around his head and shoulders which meant he was gifted psychically.

Although Bill declined the offer, that evening shook him and made him realise that all the odd things he had experienced since his childhood had an explanation – not one he could readily accept at first – but he did come to accept it in later years.

As a young boy, he would often lie awake at night watching the tiny spheres of green light flying around his room; the teenage girl who appeared by the front window and smiled at him before fading away; the elderly gentleman – whom nobody else could see – who would sit on the back lawn and watch Bill as he played with his friends.

Some years later, his mother asked Bill about the old man. She told him that she and her husband had become worried about their young son and his 'visions'; it is quite common for an only child to invent invisible playmates as a substitute for friends, but the young lad always had plenty of them. Bill was quite certain that the old man was there. He never talked. He just sat there and watched Bill and his friends playing together.

And these odd things have continued to occur to this day. While they have often unnerved him, he has never been truly frightened by them. He says that fear usually comes from within the person who experiences something – and only because they don't know how to interpret the experience or how to deal with it.

His parents weren't the only ones who were spooked by Bill's experiences – other non-psychic friends have often experienced the same things at the same time, and become quite distressed.

Bill remembers one incident as a teenager, sitting on the settee at his parents' home with Audrey, his then girlfriend, watching the television. Suddenly the pet cat leaped off the armchair with a squeal which made them both jump. He remembers telling Audrey that her neck and shoulders would soon become very cold – it had happened to the cat's – it was happening to him now, and it would shortly happen to her. He told her not to worry, as there was nothing to fear. However, as soon as the icy sensation reached her, she started to her feet with a scream and shot from the room. It took Bill quite some time to calm her down, eventually having to explain it as a poor heating system in the house, before she would agree to return!

Bill told me he had not, until recently, tried to contact a spirit – they have always contacted him – and adds that the bad thing about being psychic is like being in the Emergency Services: you are on call twenty-four hours a day. He points out that mediums quite often hold 'development circles' for anyone who is either just generally interested in spiritualism, or perhaps even someone who wants to develop their psychic ability. While some people are born psychic, most people can learn how to harness that energy which lies dormant within all of us. Yet he points out that while you can develop yourself psychically, you cannot rid yourself of the ability – it is a one-way ticket!

The house just outside Hull that Bill and his wife, Maureen, have lived in for the past six years is a perfectly normal, modest terraced house – in the physical sense. In psychical terms it is, he says, 'more like Hampton Court Maze'. While you can measure the physical width of a room in yards and feet, the psychical world cannot be measured at all. Time and distance are meaningless here. There are different levels or 'planes' of existence, and while you may sense there is someone standing there one minute – and that they are gone the next – they may not have necessarily moved away. It's just that the mind often switches between different levels and can only detect something which appears on that level.

Within the first week of moving in, odd occurrences were noted. Objects such as cutlery would keep disappearing and then turn up a few days later in the strangest places, which you could not put down to anything other than the paranormal. A fork from the silver set they received as a wedding gift turned up on top of the metal dustbin lid in the back garden. Knocks and raps were often heard on the living room ceiling, when there was no one upstairs.

Maureen still experiences the sudden chills which come and go with alarming frequency even in very warm weather. She used to experience them only when Bill was with her, but now she feels them, even when he is out of the house. Maureen says that it is almost as if the 'presence' affects her, as if it has now come to accept that she is a permanent part of Bill's life.

The odd thing which they have both heard every other night is the sound of footsteps climbing the stairs from the front door, walking past their bedroom door, and going to the spare room. Several times they have investigated, but now they just ignore it. Maureen jokes that as the couple don't have children, it often feels as if there is another unseen 'family' living in the same house as them – and as they have never been in the least bit threatening, she would be quite upset if they moved out!

Only recently, Bill has considered training to be a medium, so he can fully understand and use his psychic ability, which he always shunned in his younger years. He has even tried to contact the spirit – if spirit it be that passes through a wall into the house next door. He is quite sure the family who live there have not experienced this haunting, but he would be interested to learn more about who it might be. Whenever he senses the spirit moving through, he puts his hand to the wall, and it often feels warm.

Bill attempted to explain to me what psychic vibrations or impressions are, comparing them to radio waves. Imagine travelling back 100 years in time, he says, and explaining to someone the theory of producing and transmitting radio waves. Just consider how that would sound to them – you would be ridiculed – and yet today we take them for granted. You can't see them, you can't touch them, you can't physically interfere with their transmission, and yet these invisible, undetectable messages are all around us. In order to pick them up you need a receiver – like a radio or TV. Similarly, mediums are receivers of psychic messages.

Some people say that haunted houses are few and far between. Bill thinks that most houses previously 'lived-in', are haunted – and yet as the occupants are not usually psychic, they cannot tune into that energy or wavelength. He says that the number of times he has visited someone's house, purely on a social or business call, and seen (or more usually sensed) a spirit standing behind them, with the householders blissfully unaware of their existence, is quite staggering. And, of course, he hasn't told them for fear of scaring them – unless the apparition has seemed particularly distressed.

Bill Adamson has never been afraid of the odd things which happen to him; he just takes them in his stride. He says that everything which happens in life is natural – if it wasn't natural then it wouldn't happen. He accepts them as normal because he finds that this is the best way to deal with them, and that the only reasons we use the terms 'paranormal' or 'supernatural' is because we don't know exactly what these things are or why they happen.

He says that he is very happy with the life that he shares with Maureen and would be quite content with that on its own but his psychic ability adds a further dimension to his life which he would greatly miss if he ever lost it.

Index

127

Street by Street

HIGH WYC[OMBE]

AMERSHAM, BEACONSFIELD, MARLOW

Bourne End, Chalfont St Giles, Chalfont St Peter, Chesham,
Flackwell Heath, Gerrards Cross, Great Missenden,
Holmer Green, Little Chalfont, Marlow Bottom,
Naphill, Wooburn

1st edition September 2002

© Automobile Association Developments
Limited 2002

Ordnance Survey® This product includes map
data licensed from Ordnance
Survey® with the permission
of the Controller of Her Majesty's Stationery Office.
© Crown copyright 2002. All rights reserved.
Licence No: 399221.

Published by AA Publishing (a trading name of
Automobile Association Developments
Limited, whose registered office is Millstream,
Maidenhead Road, Windsor, Berkshire SL4 5GD.
Registered number 1878835).

The Post Office is a registered trademark of Post
Office Ltd. in the UK and other countries.

Schools address data provided by Education Direct.

One-way street data provided by:

Tele Atlas ◀ © Tele Atlas N.V.

Mapping produced by the Cartographic
Department of The Automobile Association. A01100

A CIP Catalogue record for this book is
available from the British Library.

Printed by GRAFIASA S.A., Porto, Portugal

Ref: ML191

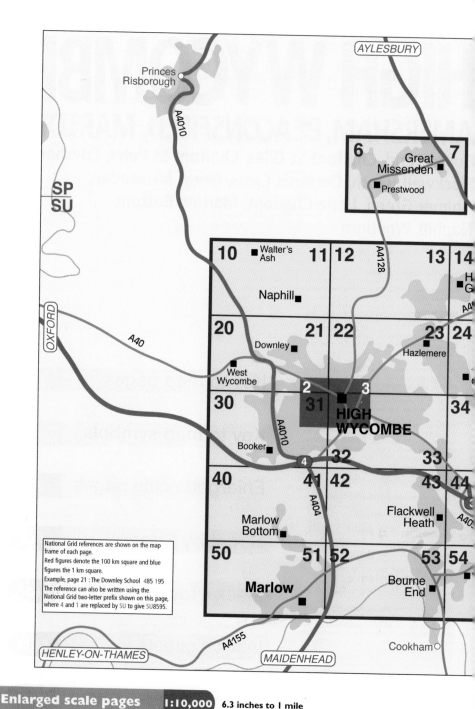

AYLESBURY

Princes Risborough

A4010

SP
SU

6   Great Missenden   7
   Prestwood

10   ■ Walter's Ash   11 | 12   A4128   13 | 14

H G

Naphill ■

OXFORD

A40

20   21 | 22   23 | 24

Downley ■

Hazlemere

West Wycombe ■

30   2   3   34

31   HIGH WYCOMBE

A4010

Booker ■

4   32   33

40   41 | 42   43 | 44

A404

Flackwell Heath ■

A40

Marlow Bottom ■

National Grid references are shown on the map frame of each page.
Red figures denote the 100 km square and blue figures the 1 km square.
Example, page 21 : The Downley School 485 195
The reference can also be written using the National Grid two-letter prefix shown on this page, where 4 and 1 are replaced by SU to give SU8595.

50   51 | 52   53 | 54

Marlow   Bourne End

A4155   Cookham ○

HENLEY-ON-THAMES   MAIDENHEAD

Enlarged scale pages   1:10,000   6.3 inches to 1 mile

0   1/4   miles   1/2
0   1/4   1/2   kilometres   3/4   1

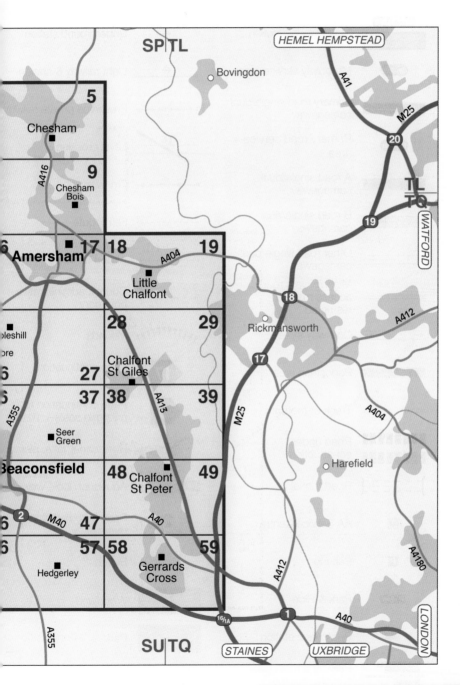

SP|TL

HEMEL HEMPSTEAD

Bovingdon

A41

M25

5

Chesham

20

A416

9

Chesham
Bois

TL
TQ

19

WATFORD

17 **18**

Amersham

A404

19

Little
Chalfont

18

28

29

Rickmansworth

A412

leshill

ore

17

27

Chalfont
St Giles

37 **38**

A413

39

A355

M25

A404

Seer
Green

Harefield

Beaconsfield

48 Chalfont
St Peter

49

2

M40 **47**

A40

57 **58**

59

Hedgerley

Gerrards
Cross

A412

A4180

16/1A

1

A40

LONDON

A355

SU|TQ

STAINES

UXBRIDGE

4.2 inches to 1 mile   **Scale of main map pages 1:15,000**

| 0 | | 1/4 | miles | 1/2 | | 3/4 | | 1 |
| 0 | 1/4 | 1/2 | kilometres | 3/4 | 1 | | 1 1/4 | 1 1/2 |

iv

Junction 9	Motorway & junction	⊖	Underground station
Services	Motorway service area	⊖	Light railway & station
	Primary road single/dual carriageway	+++++++++	Preserved private railway
Services	Primary road service area	LC	Level crossing
	A road single/dual carriageway	•—•—•—•	Tramway
	B road single/dual carriageway	----------	Ferry route
	Other road single/dual carriageway	··············	Airport runway
	Minor/private road, access may be restricted	—·—·—·—	County, administrative boundary
← ←	One-way street	ᵛᵛᵛᵛᵛᵛᵛᵛᵛ	Mounds
	Pedestrian area	**17**	Page continuation 1:15,000
============	Track or footpath	**3**	Page continuation to enlarged scale 1:10,000
	Road under construction		River/canal, lake, pier
⊢ ‒ ‒ ‒ ⊣	Road tunnel		Aqueduct, lock, weir
AA	AA Service Centre	465 ▲ Winter Hill	Peak (with height in metres)
P	Parking		Beach
P+	Park & Ride		Woodland
	Bus/coach station		Park
	Railway & main railway station		Cemetery
	Railway & minor railway station		Built-up area

	Featured building		Abbey, cathedral or priory
	City wall	**X**	Castle
A&E	Hospital with 24-hour A&E department		Historic house or building
PO	Post Office	Wakehurst Place NT	National Trust property
	Public library	**M**	Museum or art gallery
i	Tourist Information Centre		Roman antiquity
	Petrol station Major suppliers only		Ancient site, battlefield or monument
†	Church/chapel		Industrial interest
	Public toilets		Garden
	Toilet with disabled facilities		Arboretum
PH	Public house AA recommended		Farm or animal centre
	Restaurant AA inspected		Zoological or wildlife collection
	Theatre or performing arts centre		Bird collection
	Cinema		Nature reserve
	Golf course	**V**	Visitor or heritage centre
▲	Camping AA inspected		Country park
	Caravan Site AA inspected		Cave
	Camping & caravan site AA inspected		Windmill
	Theme park		Distillery, brewery or vineyard

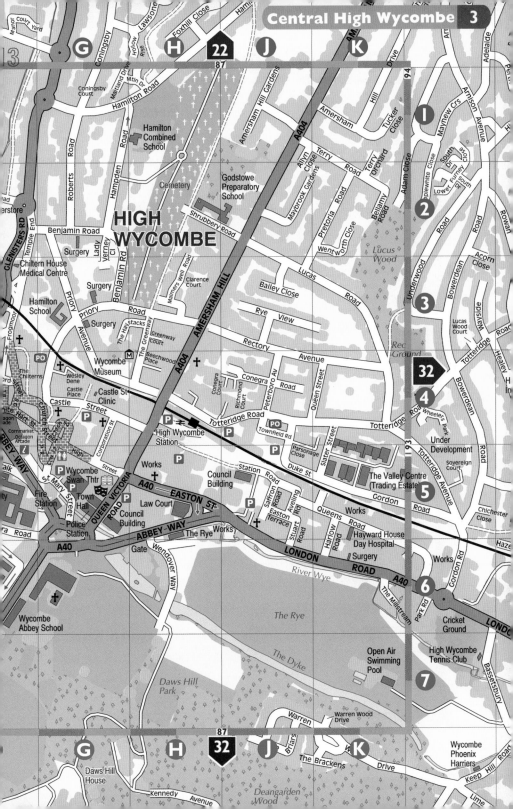

8

Pednormead End

Dawes Cl
Wev
La
Germains Close
chessbury
Rd
Delmeade
Road
Fuller's

A **B** MISS**DEN** **4** 95 RC **C** **D**

494
10

Ryecroft Road
Chessbury Road
Fuller's Hill
Close

Halfway House
Farm

1

White's
Wood

White House
Farm

2

Fuller's Hill

200

Weedon Hill
Farm

Weedon Hill

Mayhall
Farm

Our L
Catho
Prima

3

Oakway

The Willows

Mayhall L

Deep
Acres

Bois
Avenue

A

4

199

Weedonhill
Wood

Amersham
& Chiltern
RFC

Weedon Lane

Woodfield Park

H

Berry Fld

Pin
Clos

Ash
Grove
Windmill
Wood

Windmill
Wood

Butler's
Close

Reading
Drive

5

494
A4
A413

95

A **B** **16** **C** **D**

Amersh

1 grid square represents 500 metres

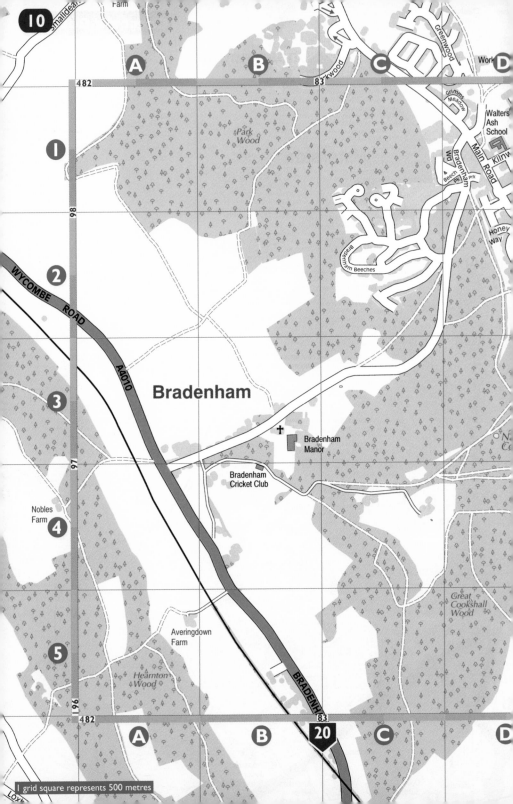

E F G H

89 90

Works

I

98

Copes
Farm

Spurlands
End

Watchet Lane

Howe
Hill
Lane

2

Langley
Farm

reat
ngshill

Heath End Road

Heath
End
Close

The
Coppice

St Margaret's CV

Copes Road

Spurlands End Road

Hawbushes
Farm

Windmill Lane

Dormer Lane

Beech Tree Road

The Rosary

Stevens Glebe
Cl Cl

3

Holmer Green
Upper School

Holmer Pl

14

Holmer Green
First School

Snowdrop Way

Honeysuckle Rd

Primrose Hill

Cowslip Road

Windmill
Drive

Haines Rd

LW

HW

Todd Cl

Watchet La

Harries Way

Fox Road

Browns Road

Cables Meadow

Orchard

Skimmers Fld

4

George's Hill

Columbine Road

Sunny Bank

Heath
Close

Brackley Dr

Wycombe Road

Copners Way

Copners Dr

Parsons Walk

Larkspur Wy

Marigold Wk

Campion
Road

Candytuft
Green

Brackley Road

Cherry
Way

Orch End

Surgery

Dean Way

Widmer
nd

Eastcourt

Dashfield
GV

Brimmers

Widmer End
Combined
School

Hill

Upper Lodge Lane

New Tree Drive

Western Dene

Lower Lodge Lane

Farndale
Gdns

Southfield

The Rise

Cherry
Way

The Orch

Hill

Laceys Drive

Nightingale
Close

Sanctuary Rd

Kestrel
Cl

Way

Badger

Inkerman

5

Inkerman
Fm

HP15

Roberts

Copes
Shroves

Cedar

Maurice
Rd

Fk F

Ride

Sawpit

Hill Avenue

Swallow
Drive

Pheasants
Dr

Chestnut
Lane

Maxwell
Dr

Hazlemere
View

Inkerman Drive

Shepherds Lane

Cedar
Park
School

The
Warren

Avenue

Clauds
Cl

PO

The
Link

Surgery

First
School

Toms Turn

Mead

Road

Eastern Dene

Green

Park Lane

AMERSHAM ROAD

A404

Golf Course

E F G H

Grange
Farm

89

23

90

96

97

Beaumont Way

Holmer

Lester
Grove

Quer

Hazlemere

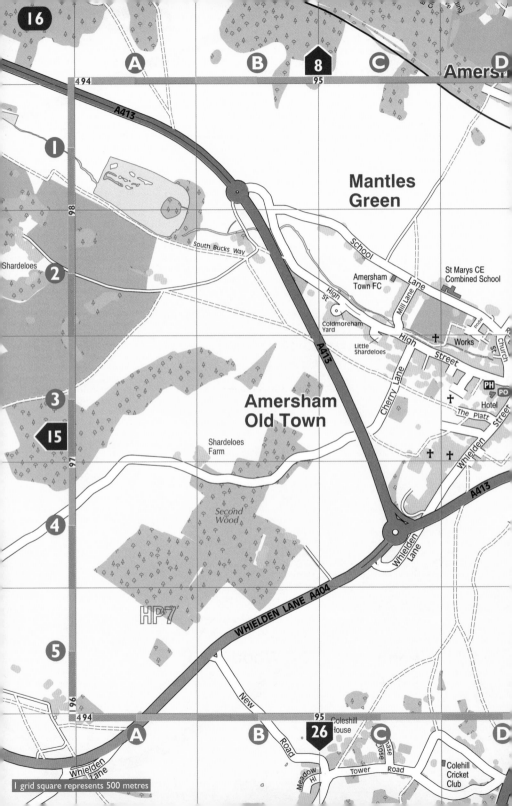

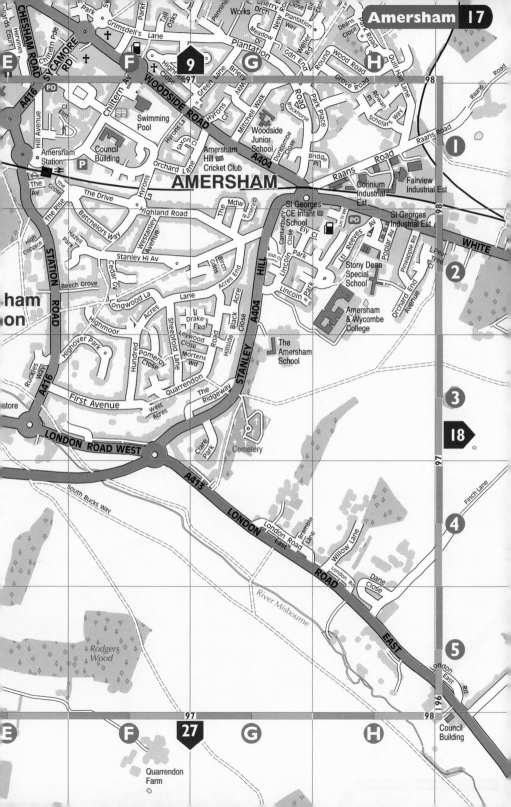

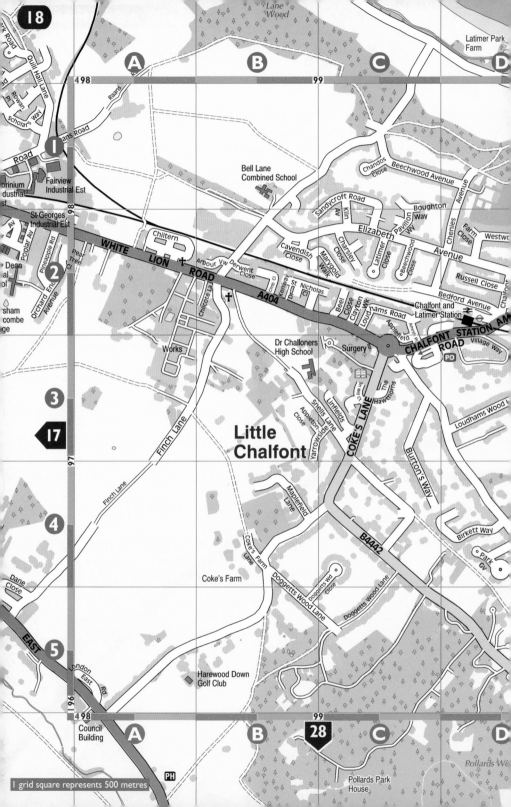

Inkerman Farm

24

Inkerman Drive

A404

A **B** **14** **C** **Pen D**
91 **Woo**

490 96

Golf C **1**

Hazlemere
Golf &
Country Club

Elder
Way

B474 **2**

Brock
Field
Close

Wellfield

Wellfield

Fitts Close

Tylers
Crs

Rushmoor Av 95

Tylers
Road

Tudor
Road

Curzon Av

Copdice

Clayfields

HAZLEMERE ROAD

Chilton
Close

Burrows Close

3

Manor Farm
Primary
School

Hartwell
Close

Larch
Close

Larch
Farm
Road

Old Kiln
Road

Works

**Tylers
Green**

23

Hawthorn
Crs

Birch Wy

Oaktre
Close

Ashley

West Av

Cherry
Tree
Way

B474

Common Woo

Kings
Ride

Kings Ride

The Chase

The
Glade

Drive

The
Chase

Meadow Walk

The
Larchlands

Johns
Close

The Green

The
Pines

Nash Pl

Kite Wood Rd

Rays
Lane

Road

4

Kite
Wood

Hillcroft Rd

The Dell

Russell

New

ELM ROAD

The
Spinneys

Johns
Road

St John's
Av

Long
Orch

Torch

PO

Surgery

Bank

School Rd

**Puttenham
Place Farm**

ngswood
Av

5

Tylers Gree
Junior
School

Lancaster
Ride

Ashwells Mnr
Dr

Church

St Cl

Gibl

Road

Glebe

St Cl

Finch
End

Carter Walk

Tylers
Green Infant
School

Penn

Ashwells

Penn
School

A **B** **34** **C** **D**
91
CHURCH ROAD
B474

npits

Lane

Ashley Lane

Beacon

Cemetery

1 grid square represents 500 metres

Chancellors

Penn Street

Woodrow

† E F **15** G H I

93 94 96

Industrial Estate

PH

Whielden

Winchmore Hill Cricket Club

Penn House

Horsemoor

Nelson Cl

The Hill

Pond Close

†

Fagnall La

PO

Winchmore Hill

Coleshill

2

95

Lane

Fagnall Lane

Fagnall Farm

3

Lane

26

Sam

Glory Farm

4

Hertfo House

Marrod's Bottom

194

5

93 94

E F **35** G H

Witheridge Wood

Seagrave's Farm

BRIDGE

Rodgers Wood

London East Rd

Council Building

E **F** **17** **G** **H**

97 98 96

I

Quarrendon Farm

Lower Bottom House Farm **2**

95

Brentford Grange

Farm La

Bottom House

Upper Bottom House **3**

28

Bottom House

Hill

Works Farm **4**

Hill Farm House

94 Lane

Bottrells **5**

Lane

CHALFONT ST GILES

E **F** **37** **G** **H**

97 98

dgemoor ods

Whit

Rise

Dean

PH Way

Three

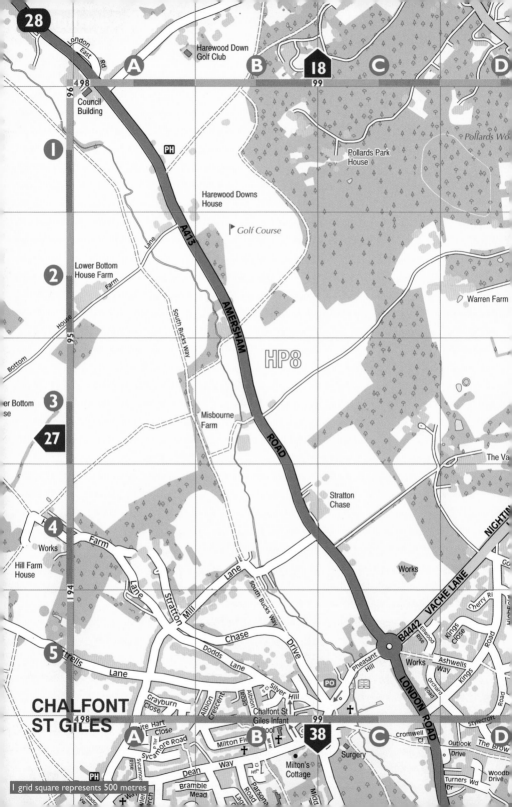

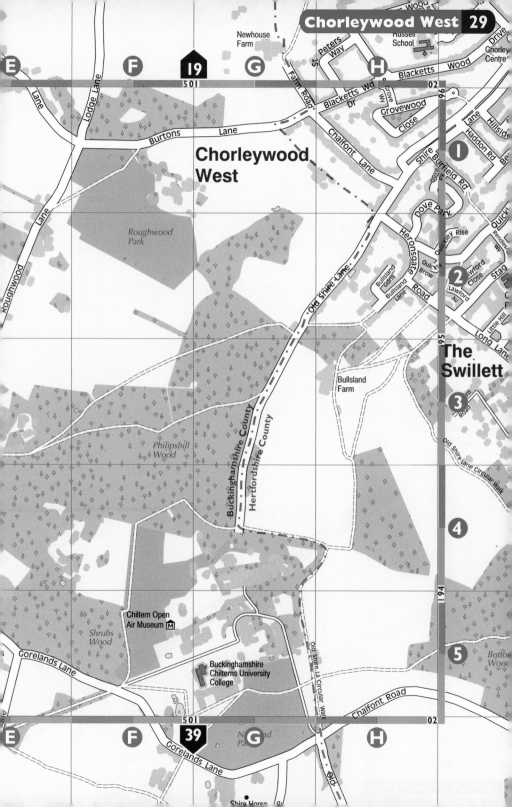

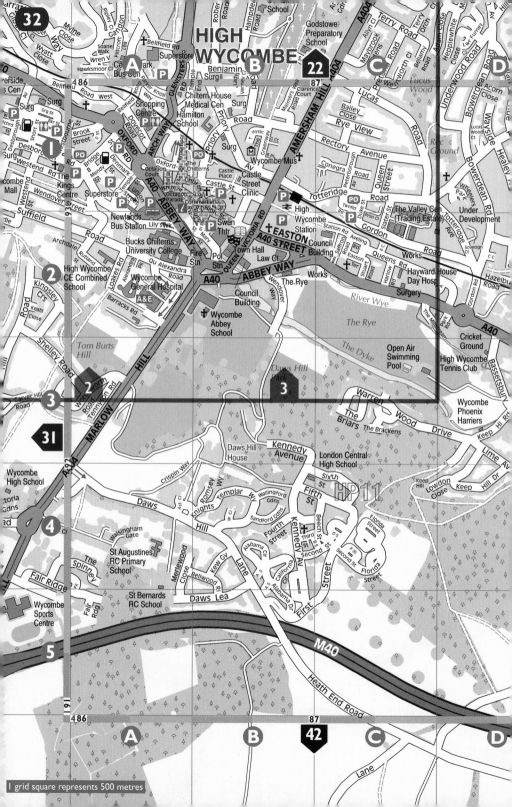

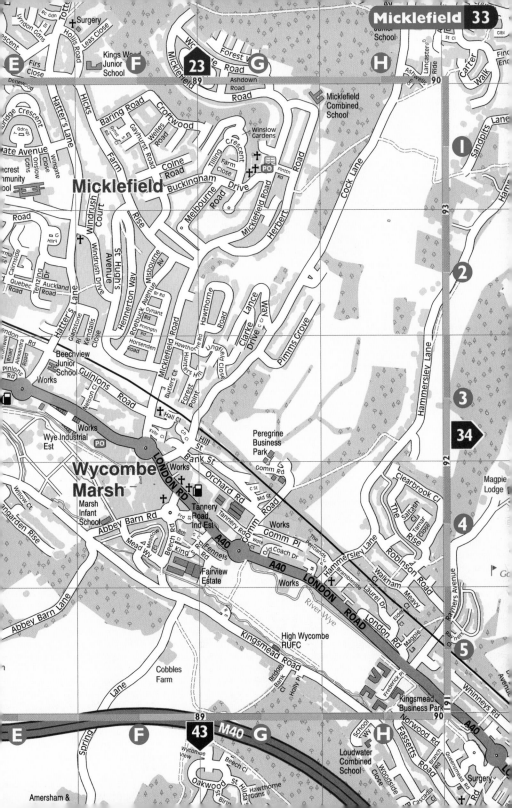

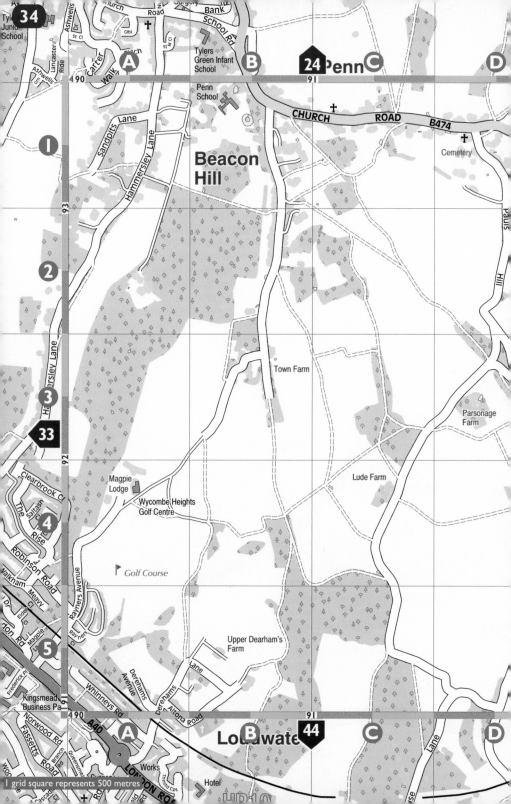

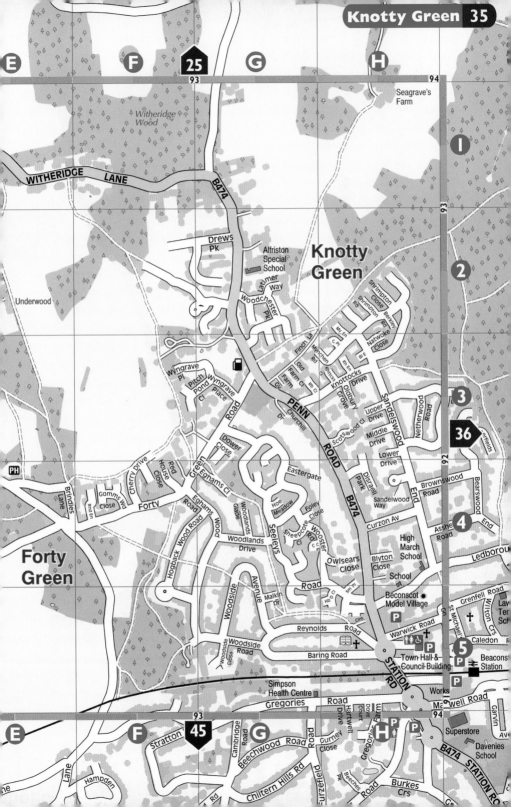

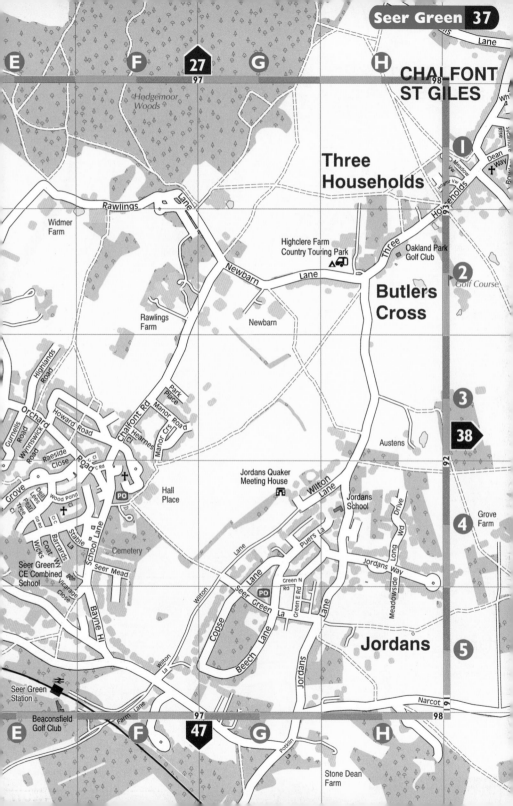

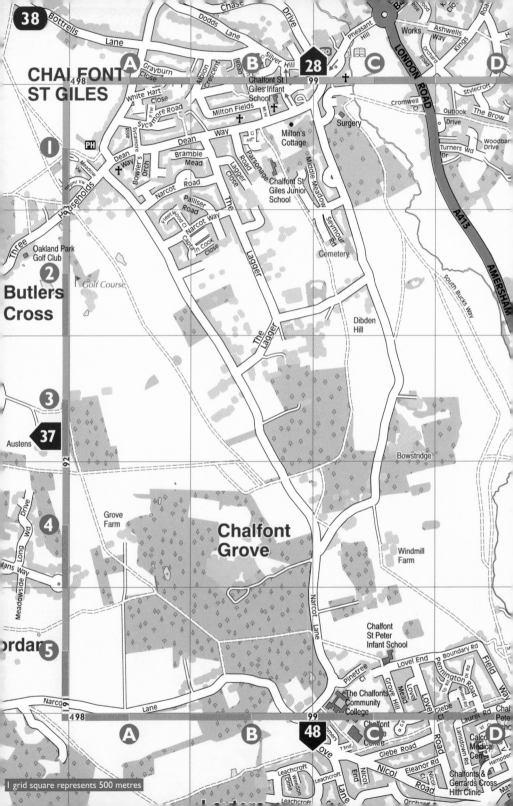

40

A   B   **30**   C   D

4 82

91

Newmer Lane
Linner Lane
Cressex Rd
Thel
Paddocks
Booker
Pl
Booker
Pl

Clay Lane
Farm

Wycombe
● Air Park

High Wycombe
Squash Club

Claymoor

Clay Lane

Clayhill

Clay

1

2

90

Beacon Lane

Beacon
Farm

Red Barn Farm

3

B482

Bluey's
Farm

4

89

Widmere Lane

Widmere
Farm

MARLOW

Cold

5

Frieth Road

Shillingridge
Wood

ROAD

High Rews

4 82

83

A   B   **50**   C   D

Mundaydean

.py
.arm

Mundaydean
Bottom

1 grid square represents 500 metres

High Wycombe RUFC

Kingsmead Road

Cobbles Farm

Lane

Bridge Bank Cl
Holly Pl
Brick Pl

E

F

33
89

G

H

Kingsmead Business P 90

A40

A40

Lo

I Surgery

PO

Birfiel

Norwood Rd

Station Rd

Queens

Willow Wy

Cascadia

Branch

shakeley

Boundary Rd

Treadaway Bus Cen

Loudwater Combined School

School Wy

Fassetts Road

Woodside Close

Bay Tree Cl

St Peters Cl

M40

Wycombe View

Oakwood

St Hilda's Wy

Hawthorne Gdns

Birinus

Beech Cl

Amersham & Wycombe College

Seymour Close

Ring Rd

Rugwood Road

Woodla e Wd Cl

Bernards Wy

Buckingham Way

Oakland Way

Fennels

Fennels Way

Fennels Farm Road

2

Treadaway Hill

Flackwell Heath Golf Club

Fairview La

Heath End Rd

Magple La

Magple Cl

Southfield Rd

Junior School

Halls Corner

Swains Lane

Treadaway Rd

N Links Rd

Knaves Busine

Carrington Primary School

Common Rd

PO

The Common

Links Ap

The Meadow

3

New Farm

Sheepridge Lane

Chapel Road

Old Kiln Road

Cherrywood Gardens

Straight

Clay

Links Wy

Links Rd

Sheepridge

Carrington Av

Highlea Avenue

Sedgmoor

Highfield Road

Sedgmoor Gdns

Hedley Rd

Bit

44

School

Cm Gn

Sedgmoor Road

River Vw

Chiltterns Cl

Highlands

Greenlands

Norland Dr

Straight

strathcona Cl

Flackwell Heath

Sedgmoor Close

Cherry Rd

The Orchard

Churchill Cl

4

Northern W

Becks

Kings Way

Ph

Parkview

Cherry Cv

Cherry Cl

Green Dragon Lane

Home Meadow Drive

Chapman Lane

Bracken Wy

Blind Lane

Pigeon House Farm

Woodside Ap
Woodside

Little Close

Willow Cl

Wilfrids W

5

Sheepridge Lane

The Close

Drive

E n

F

53
89

Chapman Lane

G

Telston Close

ourne Close

H

A4155

Well End

Chapman Lane

Clayton

Combined

Islington Road

Gree

Cliffords Wy

Avalon

Northern Hts

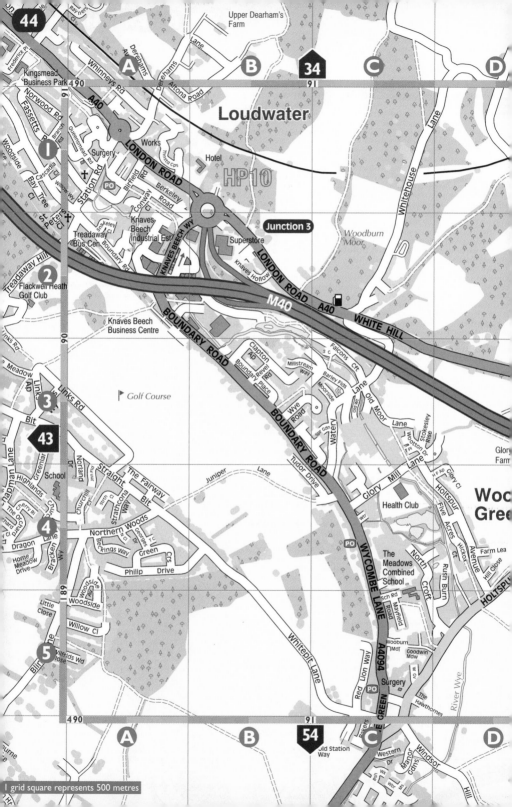

Green Lion

E

Beaconsfield Golf Club

Wilton La

Farm Lane

F

37

97

Beech Lane

G

Jordans

Narcot

H

98

16

I

Stone Dean Farm

Potkiln La

2

90

Stampwell Farm

Potkiln Lane

ON ROAD A40

3

48

rds

4

Lane

Mumfo Farm

T H

Hotel

OXFOR

189

Chiltern Hundreds

5

Common Lane

E

F

57

97

Hedgerley Lane

G

H

98

Moat Farm

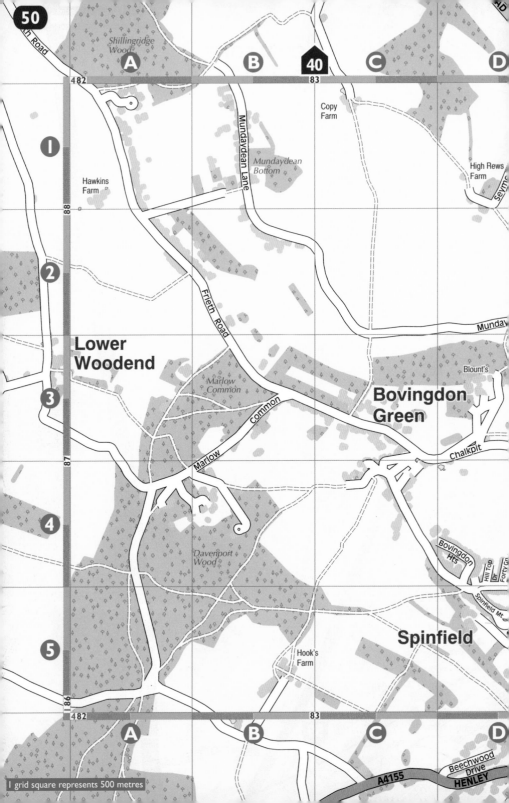

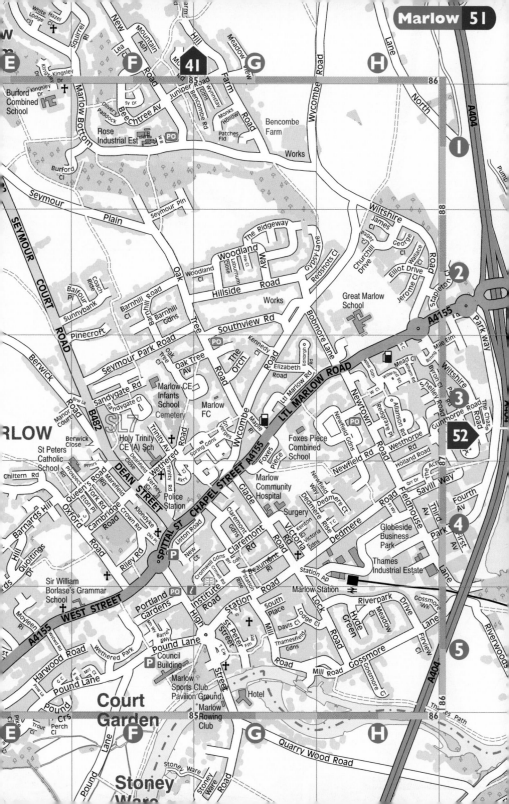

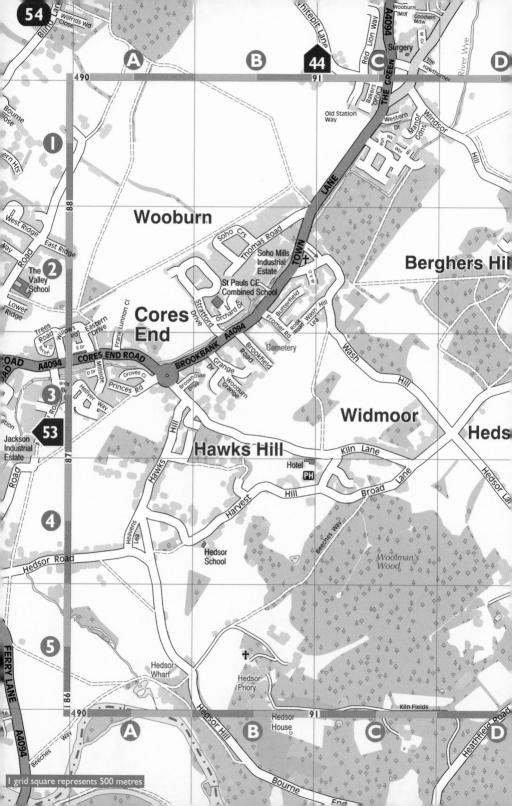

Over's Farm

● Rare Breeds

E **F** **45**
93

Lillyfee Farm

Lillyfee Farm Lane

Dipple Wood

G **H** **94**

I

Woodlands Farm

88

Green Common Lane **2**

Ship Hill

Odds Farm

Wooburn Common

Sheepcote Farm

3

56

87

Hicknham Farm

Park Lane

4 Abbey Park Farm

Wooburn Common Road

Hales Cott

Dropmore Infant School

Boveney

Wood Lane

Little Road

Dorney Wood Road

Lane

Abbey

Beeches Way

5

86

Littleworth Common

Dropmore

Common

E **F** **G** **H**
93 Horseshoe Hill 94

Brook End Farm

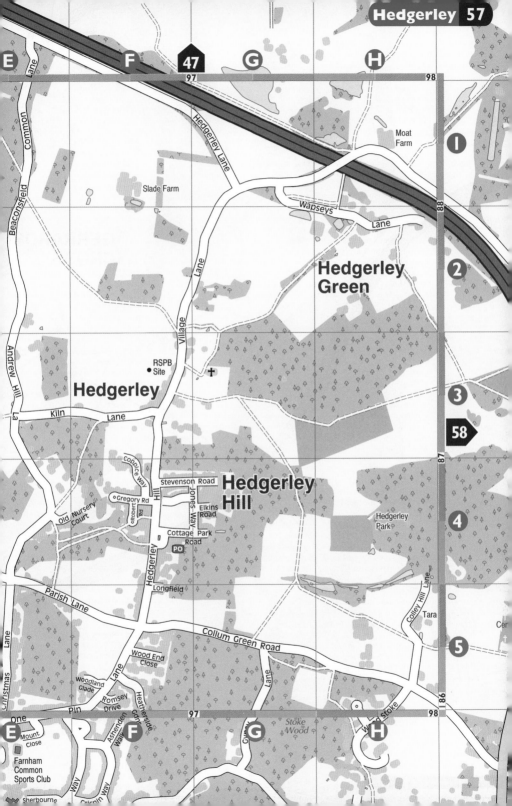

E F 47 G H

97 98

Hedgerley Lane

Moat Farm

I

88

Slade Farm

Beaconsfield Common Lane

Wapseys Lane

Hedgerley Green

2

Andrew Hill La

RSPB Site

Hedgerley

Kiln Lane

3

58

87

Coppice Way

Stevenson Road

Hedgerley Hill

Gregory Rd

Robert Rd

Hill

Jones Way

Elkins Road

Cottage Park Road

Hedgerley Park

4

Old Nursery Court

PO

Hedgerley Lane

Longfield

Parish Lane

Colley Hill Lane

Tara

5

Collum Green Road

Cer

Lane

Wood End Close

Christmas Lane

Woodland Glade

Pin

Romsey Drive

Heatherside

Ashenden Way

Gorse

Lane

Gray's Lane

Stoke Wood

Wood Stoke

86

97 98

E F G H

Mount Close

one

Farnham Common Sports Club

Way

Crispin Way

Sherbourne

58

A   B   **48**   C   D

498   99

Bulstrode
Park

Main Drive

W Cmmn

Hotel

Moat
Far

I

Valley Way

Woodbank Avenue

Donnay Close

Lane

**GERRARDS
CROSS**

2

B41

Hedgerley Lane

Wayside Gdns

WINDSOR ROAD

Me

3

Dukes Wood Drive

High

Dukes Kiln Drive

57

B'

87

Mount Hill Lane

Howards Thicket

Hedgerley
Park

4

Dukes Valley

M40

Howards W

Colley Hill Lane

Tara

Cemetery

Low
Farm

5

od Stoke

186

498   99

Fulmer
Chase

A   B   C   D

Bickeridge

Hay Lane

od Stoke

Common Road

1 grid square represents 500 metres

Fulmer

USING THE STREET INDEX

Street names are listed alphabetically. Each street name is followed by its postal town or area locality, the Postcode District, the page number, and the reference to the square in which the name is found.

Standard index entries are shown as follows:

Abbey Barn La *WYM* HP11 ....**33** E5

Street names and selected addresses not shown on the map due to scale restrictions are shown in the index with an asterisk:

The Abbey *BNEND* * SL8 ....**53** F2

GENERAL ABBREVIATIONS

ACC ...ACCESS	E ...EAST	LDG ...LODGE	R ...
ALY ...ALLEY	EMB ...EMBANKMENT	LGT ...LIGHT	RBT ...RO
AP ...APPROACH	EMBY ...EMBASSY	LK ...LOCK	RD ...
AR ...ARCADE	ESP ...ESPLANADE	LKS ...LAKES	RDG ...
ASS ...ASSOCIATION	EST ...ESTATE	LNDG ...LANDING	REP ...
AV ...AVENUE	EX ...EXCHANGE	LTL ...LITTLE	RES ...
BCH ...BEACH	EXPY ...EXPRESSWAY	LWR ...LOWER	RFC ...RUGBY FOO
BLDS ...BUILDINGS	EXT ...EXTENSION	MAG ...MAGISTRATE	RI ...
BND ...BEND	F/O ...FLYOVER	MAN ...MANSIONS	RP ...
BNK ...BANK	FC ...FOOTBALL CLUB	MD ...MEAD	RW ...
BR ...BRIDGE	FK ...FORK	MDW ...MEADOWS	S ...
BRK ...BROOK	FLD ...FIELD	MEM ...MEMORIAL	SCH ...
BTM ...BOTTOM	FLDS ...FIELDS	MKT ...MARKET	SE ...
BUS ...BUSINESS	FLS ...FALLS	MKTS ...MARKETS	SER ...SE
BVD ...BOULEVARD	FLS ...FLATS	ML ...MALL	SH ...
BY ...BYPASS	FM ...FARM	ML ...MILL	SHOP ...
CATH ...CATHEDRAL	FT ...FORT	MNR ...MANOR	SKWY ...
CEM ...CEMETERY	FWY ...FREEWAY	MS ...MEWS	SMT ...
CEN ...CENTRE	FY ...FERRY	MSN ...MISSION	SOC ...
CFT ...CROFT	GA ...GATE	MT ...MOUNT	SP ...
CH ...CHURCH	GAL ...GALLERY	MTN ...MOUNTAIN	SPR ...
CHA ...CHASE	GDN ...GARDEN	MTS ...MOUNTAINS	SQ ...
CHYD ...CHURCHYARD	GDNS ...GARDENS	MUS ...MUSEUM	ST ...
CIR ...CIRCLE	GLD ...GLADE	MWY ...MOTORWAY	STN ...
CIRC ...CIRCUS	GLN ...GLEN	N ...NORTH	STR ...
CL ...CLOSE	GN ...GREEN	NE ...NORTH EAST	STRD ...
CLFS ...CLIFFS	GND ...GROUND	NW ...NORTH WEST	SW ...S
CMP ...CAMP	GRA ...GRANGE	O/P ...OVERPASS	TDG ...
CNR ...CORNER	GRG ...GARAGE	OFF ...OFFICE	TER ...
CO ...COUNTY	GT ...GREAT	ORCH ...ORCHARD	THWY ...TH
COLL ...COLLEGE	GTWY ...GATEWAY	OV ...OVAL	TNL ...
COM ...COMMON	GV ...GROVE	PAL ...PALACE	TOLL ...
COMM ...COMMISSION	HGR ...HIGHER	PAS ...PASSAGE	TPK ...
CON ...CONVENT	HL ...HILL	PAV ...PAVILION	TR ...
COT ...COTTAGE	HLS ...HILLS	PDE ...PARADE	TRL ...
COTS ...COTTAGES	HO ...HOUSE	PH ...PUBLIC HOUSE	TWR ...
CP ...CAPE	HOL ...HOLLOW	PK ...PARK	U/P ...
CPS ...COPSE	HOSP ...HOSPITAL	PKWY ...PARKWAY	UNI ...
CR ...CREEK	HRB ...HARBOUR	PL ...PLACE	UPR ...
CREM ...CREMATORIUM	HTH ...HEATH	PLN ...PLAIN	V ...
CRS ...CRESCENT	HTS ...HEIGHTS	PLNS ...PLAINS	VA ...
CSWY ...CAUSEWAY	HVN ...HAVEN	PLZ ...PLAZA	VIAD ...
CT ...COURT	HWY ...HIGHWAY	POL ...POLICE STATION	VIL ...
CTRL ...CENTRAL	IMP ...IMPERIAL	PR ...PRINCE	VIS ...
CTS ...COURTS	IN ...INLET	PREC ...PRECINCT	VLG ...
CTYD ...COURTYARD	IND EST ...INDUSTRIAL ESTATE	PREP ...PREPARATORY	VLS ...
CUTT ...CUTTINGS	INF ...INFIRMARY	PRIM ...PRIMARY	VW ...
CV ...COVE	INFO ...INFORMATION	PROM ...PROMENADE	W ...
CYN ...CANYON	INT ...INTERCHANGE	PRS ...PRINCESS	WD ...
DEPT ...DEPARTMENT	IS ...ISLAND	PRT ...PORT	WHF ...
DL ...DALE	JCT ...JUNCTION	PT ...POINT	WK ...
DM ...DAM	JTY ...JETTY	PTH ...PATH	WKS ...
DR ...DRIVE	KG ...KING	PZ ...PIAZZA	WLS ...
DRO ...DROVE	KNL ...KNOLL	QD ...QUADRANT	WY ...
DRY ...DRIVEWAY	L ...LAKE	QU ...QUEEN	YD ...
DWGS ...DWELLINGS	LA ...LANE	QY ...QUAY	YHA ...YOU

CODE TOWNS AND AREA ABBREVIATIONS

...Amersham
...Amersham south
...Beaconsfield
...Bourne End
...Chalfont St Peter/
Gerrards Cross
...Chesham

CSTG ...Chalfont St Giles
DEN/HRF ...Denham/Harefield
DTCH/LGLY ...Datchet/Langley
FLKWH ...Flackwell Heath
GTMIS/PWD ...Great Missenden/
Prestwood
HAZ/HG ...Hazlemere/Holmer Green

HWYN ...High Wycombe north
HWYW ...High Wycombe west
MDHD ...Maidenhead
MLW ...Marlow
RKW/CH/CXG ...Rickmansworth/
Chorleywood/
Croxley Green

SKCH ...Stokenchurch
SL ...Slough
SLN ...Slough north
WYM ...Wycombe Marsh

x - streets

Abb - Buc

A

La *WYM* HP11 ...**33** E5
Rd *WYM* HP11 ...**33** F4
La *SL* SL1 ...**56** A4
END SL8 ...**53** F1
NEND * SL8 ...**53** F2
MIS/PWD * HP16 ...**7** G2
YM HP11 ...**3** F4
WYW HP12 ...**31** F5
HM HP5 ...**5** E1
Av *HWYW* HP12 ...**2** A2
Dr *BNEND* SL8 ...**53** G4
YN HP13 ...**32** D1
HWYW HP12 ...**31** G4
CFSP/GDCR SL9 ...**48** D4
ISS HP7 ...**17** G2
WYN HP13 ...**21** G4
W SL7 ...**51** H4
CSHM HP5 ...**5** E2
HWYN HP13 ...**22** D5
CFSP/GDCR * SL9 ...**48** D1
WYM HP11 ...**32** B4
WYM HP11 ...**32** B4
M HP11 ...**32** B4
SHM HP5 ...**4** D3
HM HP5 ...**5** E4
STG HP8 ...**38** B1
TG HP8 ...**28** B5
2 ...**31** E3
t *CSHM* HP5 ...**5** E3
k *WYM* HP11 ...**2** E6
d *HWYN* HP13 ...**33** E3
VYW HP12 ...**31** E5
HG HP15 ...**14** A3
MLW SL7 ...**51** H3
KCH HP14 ...**11** E2
N HP13 ...**3** J2
M HP5 ...**5** E2
HAZ/HG HP15 ...**23** H2
KWH HP10 ...**34** A5
l *HWYN* HP13 ...**3** H3
Hill Dr *HWYN* HP13 ...**3** K1
Hill Gdns
3 ...**3** J1
l *AMSS* HP7 ...**18** C2
Rd *AMS* HP6 ...**8** D3
...**18** D2
...**36** C3
R SL9 ...**49** F4
...**9** E2
...**28** B2
...**38** D2
P15 ...**23** E3
Wy *AMS* HP6 ...**19** E2
M HP5 ...**4** D5
La *SLN* SL2 ...**57** E3
MLW SL7 ...**41** E3
HWYN HP13 ...**21** H4
MSS HP7 ...**18** C2
AMSS HP7 ...**18** B3
k *CSHM* HP5 ...**9** F2
a *HWYW* HP12 ...**21** E5
AMSS HP7 ...**18** B2
BEAC * HP9 ...**35** H5
M HP11 ...**2** D5
YN HP13 ...**3** F4
WYM HP11 ...**32** B4
HWYN HP13 ...**22** D4
HWYW HP12 ...**30** D3
HP14 ...**10** D2
d *HWYN* HP13 ...**23** G5
y *AMS* HP6 ...**9** F5
d *CSHM* HP5 ...**4** B1
HAZ/HG HP15 ...**23** H3
CSHM HP5 ...**5** F2
HAZ/HG HP15 ...**23** H3
HP6 ...**8** C4
FSP/GDCR SL9 ...**49** E2
KWH HP10 ...**24** A3
W HP12 ...**31** E4

Ashwells *FLKWH* HP10 ...**23** H5
Ashwells Manor Dr
FLKWH HP10 ...**23** H5
Ashwells Wy *CSTG* HP8 ...**28** C5
Assheton Rd *BEAC* HP9 ...**35** H4
Auckland Rd *HWYN* HP13 ...**33** E2
Austenway *CFSP/GDCR* SL9 ...**48** D3
Austenwood Cl *CFSP/GDCR* SL9 ...**48** C2
WYM HP11 ...**32** A4
Austenwood La *CFSP/GDCR* SL9 ...**48** D2
Avalon Rd *BNEND* SL8 ...**53** H1
Aveling Rd *HWYN* HP13 ...**3** J5
The Avenue *AMSS* HP7 ...**17** E1
BNEND SL8 ...**53** F2
Avery Av *HWYN* HP13 ...**21** F3
Aylesbury Wy *BEAC* HP9 ...**46** A2
Aylward Gdns *CSHM* HP5 ...**4** C3
Azalea Cl *HAZ/HG* HP15 ...**23** G2

B

Back La *GTMIS/PWD* HP16 ...**7** G2
The Backs *CSHM* HP5 ...**5** E4
Badgebury Ri *MLW* SL7 ...**41** E4
Badgers Wy *MLW* SL7 ...**41** E4
Badger Wy *HAZ/HG* HP15 ...**13** H5
Bailey Cl *HWYN* HP13 ...**3** J3
Bakers Orch *FLKWH* HP10 ...**54** C1
Baker St *WYM* HP11 ...**2** D3
Baldwin Rd *BEAC* HP9 ...**46** D2
Balfour Pl *MLW* SL7 ...**51** E2
Bank Rd *FLKWH* HP10 ...**24** B5
Bank St *HWYN* HP13 ...**33** F3
Barbers Wood Cl *HWYW* HP12 ...**30** D4
Baring Rd *BEAC* HP9 ...**35** G5
HWYN HP13 ...**33** F1
Barley Cl *HAZ/HG* HP15 ...**23** G2
Barley Flds *FLKWH* HP10 ...**44** C3
Barley Wy *MLW* SL7 ...**51** F5
Barnards Hl *MLW* SL7 ...**51** E4
Barn Ct *HWYW* HP12 ...**31** E1
Barnes Av *CSHM* HP5 ...**5** E3
Barnhill Cl *MLW* SL7 ...**51** F2
Barnhill Gdns *MLW* SL7 ...**51** F2
Barnhill Rd *MLW* SL7 ...**51** F2
Baronsmead Rd *HWYW* HP12 ...**2** B6
Barracks Hl *AMSS* HP7 ...**26** B3
Barracks Rd *WYM* HP11 ...**2** E6
Barrards Wy *BEAC* HP9 ...**37** E4
Barratt Pl *HWYN* * HP13 ...**3** J5
Barry Cl *HWYW* HP12 ...**31** E5
Bartons Rd *HAZ/HG* HP15 ...**23** G4
Barton Wy *HWYN* HP13 ...**23** E4
Bassetsbury La *WYM* HP11 ...**32** D3
Batchelors Wy *AMSS* HP7 ...**17** F2
CSHM HP5 ...**4** D2
Battings Wood Gdns
SKCH HP14 ...**11** E2
Bayley Gdns *SKCH* HP14 ...**11** G4
Bayne Hl *BEAC* HP9 ...**37** F5
Bay Tree Cl *WYM* HP11 ...**43** H1
Beacham Rd *HWYW* HP12 ...**41** E1
Beacon Cl *CFSP/GDCR* SL9 ...**39** E5
Beacon La *MLW* SL7 ...**40** A2
Beaconsfield Av *HWYN* HP13 ...**21** H4
Beaconsfield Common La
SLN SL2 ...**57** E2
Bealings End *BEAC* HP9 ...**35** H3
Bearswood End *BEAC* HP9 ...**36** A4
Beaufort Gdns *MLW* SL7 ...**51** G4
Beaumont Ri *MLW* SL7 ...**51** G4
Beaumont Wy *HAZ/HG* HP15 ...**23** F1
Beckings Wy *FLKWH* HP10 ...**44** A4
Bedder Rd *HWYW* HP12 ...**31** E5
Bedford Av *AMS* HP6 ...**18** C2
Bedford Cl *RKW/CH/CXG* WD3 ...**19** H1
Beech Cl *FLKWH* HP10 ...**43** G1
WYM HP11 ...**33** F4
Beech Ct *MLW* * SL7 ...**51** G4
Beechcroft Rd *CSHM* HP5 ...**4** C3
Beeches Gv *HAZ/HG* HP15 ...**23** G3

Beeches Pk *BEAC* HP9 ...**45** H1
Beeches Wy *MDHD* SL6 ...**54** C4
Beech Gv *AMSS* HP7 ...**17** E2
Beechingstoke *MLW* SL7 ...**51** H3
Beechlands *HAZ/HG* HP15 ...**23** E3
Beech La *BEAC* HP9 ...**37** G5
GTMIS/PWD HP16 ...**6** A2
Beech Pk *SKCH* HP14 ...**10** D1
Beech Rd *WYM* HP11 ...**33** F4
Beech St *WYM* HP11 ...**32** C4
Beechtree Av *MLW* SL7 ...**51** F1
Beech Tree Rd *HAZ/HG* HP15 ...**14** A3
Beech Waye *CFSP/GDCR* SL9 ...**59** F2
Beechwood Av *AMS* HP6 ...**18** C1
RKW/CH/CXG WD3 ...**19** H5
Beechwood Cl *AMS* HP6 ...**18** C2
Beechwood Pl *HWYN* HP13 ...**3** H4
Beechwood Rd *BEAC* HP9 ...**45** G1
HWYN HP13 ...**20** D3
Beel Cl *AMSS* HP7 ...**18** C2
Bellamy Rd *HWYN* HP13 ...**3** K2
Bellfield Rd *HWYN* HP13 ...**2** E3
Bellfield Rd West *HWYN* HP13 ...**2** D3
Bellingdon Rd *CSHM* HP5 ...**4** D4
Bellwood Ri *WYM* HP11 ...**32** A4
Belmont Rd *CSHM* HP5 ...**4** D2
Bench Manor Crs
CFSP/GDCR SL9 ...**48** C2
Bencombe Rd *MLW* SL7 ...**51** F1
Benham Cl *CSHM* HP5 ...**4** C3
Benjamin Rd *HWYN* HP13 ...**3** G2
Bennetts *CSHM* HP5 ...**5** F3
Bentinck Cl *CFSP/GDCR* SL9 ...**48** D5
Berkeley Av *CSHM* HP5 ...**4** B2
Berkeley Cl *CSHM* HP5 ...**4** C3
Berkeley Ms *MLW* * SL7 ...**51** H4
Berkeley Rd *FLKWH* HP10 ...**44** A1
Berkhampstead Rd *CSHM* HP5 ...**5** E3
Berkley Rd *BEAC* HP9 ...**35** H2
Bernards Cl *GTMIS/PWD* HP16 ...**7** F2
Bernards Wy *FLKWH* HP10 ...**43** G2
Berry Field Pk *AMS* HP6 ...**8** D5
Berwick Cl *BEAC* HP9 ...**46** D2
MLW SL7 ...**51** E3
Berwick La *MLW* SL7 ...**51** F3
Berwick Rd *MLW* SL7 ...**51** E3
Bevan Hl *CSHM* HP5 ...**4** D2
Bevelwood Gdns *HWYW* HP12 ...**31** F1
Beverley Cl *MLW* SL7 ...**51** E4
Birch Cl *AMS* HP6 ...**9** G5
Birchdale *CFSP/GDCR* SL9 ...**58** D3
Birches Ri *HWYN* HP13 ...**2** A1
The Birches *HWYN* HP13 ...**23** E5
Birch Gdns *AMSS* HP7 ...**17** G2
Birch St *WYM* HP11 ...**32** B4
Birch Wy *CSHM* HP5 ...**5** F2
HAZ/HG HP15 ...**23** H3
Birchwood Cha *HAZ/HG* HP15 ...**12** C1
Birchwood Cl *HWYW* HP12 ...**30** D2
Birfield Rd *FLKWH* HP10 ...**44** A1
Birinus Ct *HWYW* HP12 ...**31** E3
Birkett Wy *CSTG* HP8 ...**18** D4
Bishops Wk *FLKWH* HP10 ...**54** C1
The Bit *AMSS* * HP7 ...**26** B2
Black Acre Cl *AMSS* HP7 ...**17** G2
Blacketts Wood Dr
RKW/CH/CXG WD3 ...**19** H5
Black Horse Av *CSHM* HP5 ...**9** F1
Blackhorse Crs *AMS* HP6 ...**17** G1
Blacksmith La *GTMIS/PWD* HP16 ...**6** B3
Blackwell Hall La *CSHM* HP5 ...**9** H3
Blenheim Rd *HWYW* HP12 ...**31** F4
Blind La *BNEND* SL8 ...**53** G2
FLKWH HP10 ...**43** H5
Blucher St *CSHM* HP5 ...**4** D4
Blyton Cl *BEAC* HP9 ...**35** H4
Bobmore La *MLW* SL7 ...**51** G2
Bois Av *AMS* HP6 ...**8** D4
Bois Hl *CSHM* HP5 ...**9** F2
Bois La *AMS* HP6 ...**9** F4
Bois Moor Rd *CSHM* HP5 ...**9** E2
Bookerhill Rd *HWYW* HP12 ...**31** E3
Booker La *HWYW* HP12 ...**31** F1

Booker Pl *HWYW* HP12 ...**30** D5
Boss La *HAZ/HG* HP15 ...**12** B3
Boston Dr *BNEND* SL8 ...**53** H3
Botley Rd *CSHM* HP5 ...**5** G3
Bottom House Farm La *CSTG* HP8 **27** F4
Bottrells La *CSTG* HP8 ...**27** H5
Boughton Wy *AMS* HP6 ...**18** C2
Boundary Pl *FLKWH* HP10 ...**44** B3
Boundary Rd *CFSP/GDCR* SL9 ...**38** D5
FLKWH HP10 ...**44** A2
Bourne Cl *BNEND* SL8 ...**53** H1
Boveney Wood La *SL* SL1 ...**55** H5
Bovingdon Hts *MLW* SL7 ...**50** D4
Bowden La *WYM* HP11 ...**32** D3
Bowerdean Rd *HWYN* HP13 ...**32** D1
Bowler Lea *HWYN* HP13 ...**21** F3
Bowler's Orch *CSTG* HP8 ...**38** A1
Box Tree Cl *CSHM* * HP5 ...**9** F1
The Brackens *WYM* HP11 ...**32** C3
Bracken Wy *FLKWH* HP10 ...**43** H4
Brackenwood *SKCH* HP14 ...**11** E3
Brackley Dr *HAZ/HG* HP15 ...**13** G4
Brackley Rd *HAZ/HG* HP15 ...**13** G4
Bradcutts La *MDHD* SL6 ...**52** D5
Bradenham Beeches
SKCH HP14 ...**10** C2
Bradenham Rd *SKCH* HP14 ...**10** B5
Bradenham Wd *SKCH* HP14 ...**10** D1
Bradshaw Rd *HWYN* HP13 ...**33** F2
The Braid *CSHM* HP5 ...**5** G3
Brallings La *CFSP/GDCR* SL9 ...**39** G2
Bramble Cl *CFSP/GDCR* SL9 ...**39** E4
Bramble La *AMSS* HP7 ...**17** G4
Bramble Md *CSTG* HP8 ...**38** A1
Brambleside *FLKWH* HP10 ...**33** H4
Bramley End *GTMIS/PWD* HP16 ...**12** A2
Brampton Ms *MLW* * SL7 ...**51** F5
Branch Rd *FLKWH* HP10 ...**43** H1
Brandon Rd *HWYW* HP12 ...**30** D5
Brands Hill Av *HWYN* HP13 ...**22** C2
Brecon Wy *HWYN* HP13 ...**2** B1
Brenchwood Cl *HWYN* HP13 ...**21** E3
Brent Rd *BNEND* SL8 ...**53** G2
The Briars *HAZ/HG* HP15 ...**14** A3
WYM HP11 ...**32** C3
Briarswood *HAZ/HG* HP15 ...**23** H2
Bridge Bank Cl *WYM* HP11 ...**33** G5
Bridge Pl *AMS* HP6 ...**17** G1
Bridgestone Dr *BNEND* SL8 ...**53** H3
Bridge St *WYM* HP11 ...**2** E4
Bridle Ga *WYM* HP11 ...**2** C5
Briery Wy *AMS* HP6 ...**9** G5
Brill Cl *MLW* SL7 ...**51** E4
Brimmers Hl *HAZ/HG* HP15 ...**13** E4
Brindles La *BEAC* HP9 ...**35** E4
Brindley Av *HWYN* HP13 ...**2** C1
Britannia Rd *CSHM* HP5 ...**5** E2
Broadlands Av *CSHM* HP5 ...**5** E3
Broad La *FLKWH* HP10 ...**54** C4
Broad St *CSHM* HP5 ...**5** E3
Broadway *AMSS* HP7 ...**16** D3
Broadway Cl *AMSS* HP7 ...**16** D3
The Broadway *BEAC* * HP9 ...**35** H5
CFSP/GDCR * SL9 ...**48** D1
CSHM HP5 ...**5** E4
Brockhurst Rd *CSHM* HP5 ...**5** E2
Brookbank *FLKWH* HP10 ...**54** A3
Brooke Furmston Pl *MLW* * SL7 ...**51** G3
Brookfield Rd *FLKWH* HP10 ...**54** B3
Brookhouse Dr *BNEND* SL8 ...**54** A3
Brookside *FLKWH* * HP10 ...**44** A1
Brook St *WYM* HP11 ...**2** E3
Broombarn La *GTMIS/PWD* HP16 ...**6** D2
Broom Cl *HAZ/HG* * HP15 ...**23** G2
Broomfield Cl *GTMIS/PWD* HP16 ...**6** D2
Broomfield Hl
GTMIS/PWD HP16 ...**6** D2
Browns Rd *HAZ/HG* HP15 ...**14** A4
Brownswood Rd *BEAC* HP9 ...**35** H4
The Brow *CSTG* HP8 ...**38** D1
Brunel Rd *HWYN* HP13 ...**21** H4
Brushwood Rd *CSHM* HP5 ...**5** F2
Buckingham Cl *HWYN* * HP13 ...**33** G2

C

D

S

T

Notes

Notes

 **Street by Street** QUESTIONNAIRE

Dear Atlas User
Your comments, opinions and recommendations are very important to us.
So please help us to improve our street atlases by taking a few minutes
to complete this simple questionnaire.

You do NOT need a stamp (unless posted outside the UK). If you do not want to remove this page from your street atlas, then photocopy it or write your answers on a plain sheet of paper.

Send to: The Editor, AA Street by Street, FREEPOST SCE 4598,
Basingstoke RG21 4GY

ABOUT THE ATLAS...

Which city/town/county did you buy?
_____

Are there any features of the atlas or mapping that you find particularly useful?
_____
_____
_____

Is there anything we could have done better?
_____
_____
_____

Why did you choose an AA Street by Street atlas?
_____
_____
_____

Did it meet your expectations?

Exceeded ☐   **Met all** ☐   **Met most** ☐   **Fell below** ☐

Please give your reasons
_____
_____
_____
_____
_____

ML

continued overleaf

Where did you buy it?

For what purpose? (please tick all applicable)

To use in your own local area ☐   To use on business or at work ☐

Visiting a strange place ☐   In the car ☐   On foot ☐

Other (please state)

LOCAL KNOWLEDGE...

Local knowledge is invaluable. Whilst every attempt has been made to make the information contained in this atlas as accurate as possible, should you notice any inaccuracies, please detail them below (if necessary, use a blank piece of paper) or e-mail us at *streetbystreet@theAA.com*

ABOUT YOU...

Name (Mr/Mrs/Ms)
Address
                                                        Postcode
Daytime tel no
E-mail address

Which age group are you in?

Under 25 ☐   25-34 ☐   35-44 ☐   45-54 ☐   55-64 ☐   65+ ☐

Are you an AA member?   YES ☐   NO ☐

Do you have Internet access?   YES ☐   NO ☐

Thank you for taking the time to complete this questionnaire. Please send it to us as soon as possible, and remember, you do not need a stamp (unless posted outside the UK).

T

TRIPLE C
METHOD®

*Gain Clarity, Boost Confidence
& Gain Courage
So You Can Live Life Lit!*

R Y A N   S P E N C E

Identifiers:
ISBN 978-1-7397229-0-6 (paperback)
ISBN 978-1-7397229-1-3 (ebook)

Book editor: Catherine Turner
Book designer: Ines Monnet
Cover designer: topbookdesigner
Back cover photography: Palita Mak-Drury

First published 2022 by Take Flight Publishing

For Luca and Rafa

Life is all there is. And if that's true, then we have to really live it – we have to take it for everything it has and 'die enormous' instead of 'living dormant'.

Jay Z

CONTENTS

Note to Reader

Throughout this book there are questions posed and exercises to work through. To make it easy to do the work to get the results you're looking for, I've created a workbook to house your thoughts. To get the workbook for free visit iamryanspence.com/the-triple-c-method-book.

I invite you to read the book first, then work through the workbook, referring back to the book as needed.

PREFACE

Do you have a long-standing dream of doing something bold and audacious? Maybe something that's been on your bucket list for a while that scares and excites you in equal measure?

Writing a book has been a long-standing dream of mine. But it was always something I would do later when I had more time. So, like many people's dreams, my ambition to become an author existed as more of a hopeful wish than an intentional goal.

So what changed?

I did. Or, more specifically, my mindset and attitude changed. See, what I discovered on my personal development quest is that time is relative. We all have the same amount of time in a day, and many of the things we say we want to do but don't have time for, actually don't need to take that long. To achieve anything you want, you need to convert it from a hopeful wish to a promise – a statement of intent. A commitment to yourself that you'll get the thing done, no matter what life throws at you. In writing this book I refined this idea into a simple three-part framework for achieving your goals. It's called the D.I.D. framework, which stands for Decide, Inscribe, Describe.

Decide what your goal is. Decide why you want to achieve that goal. Decide to become the type of person who achieves that goal.

Inscribe your goal. Write it down and place it somewhere you'll see it every day like your office, your refrigerator, your bathroom mirror, or all three. The more you see your goal, the more embedded it becomes in your subconscious mind.

Describe your goal. Tell people what you're trying to do and why you're trying to do it. It's a scary thought, particularly when you don't have it all figured out yet, but there are three key reasons why telling people what you're striving for will help push you towards achieving the thing that you want.

1. Reality. When you tell people about your goal, you speak it into existence. It becomes something real instead of a vague idea floating around in your head.

2. Accountability. If people know you're up to something, they're going to ask you about it. And when you know people are going to ask you how it's going and how much progress you've made, you're going to want to get shit done to avoid the embarrassment. (I know we shouldn't care about other people's opinions, but let's face it, we all care a little.)

3. Support. When people know what you're doing, they're going to want to support you. It's a lot easier to move forward when you have a squad supporting you, willing you to succeed and cheering you on from the sidelines.

Another thing I learned in writing this book is that achieving the goal isn't really the point; it's what you learn and who you become in the process of trying to achieve that goal that truly matters. Committing to the process, even when things aren't going the way you'd like – even when, as in my case, you read the first draft of your first book and it makes you cry with how bad it is – is a masterclass in personal development that no course or book can prepare you for.

Because, as I'll share with you in this book, what I've learned through my experiences of leaping into the unknown is that there's no substitute for taking action. To find out who you are and what you're capable of, you have to be prepared to step into the arena, leave behind the veil of comfort and security, and trust you have what you need to figure things out along the way.

There were times in writing this book when I wanted to stop writing. I felt it was too big a task to write a book and get it out into the world. That inner critic that we all have inside of us sowed seeds of self-doubt in my mind with questions like, *Isn't this just a waste of time? Do you think anybody actually wants to read this? C'mon, does the world really need another book on personal development?*

You know what kept me going? It was the knowledge that the message included in this book needed to be heard. Too many people are living the life they think they should want, accepting that surviving, rather than thriving, is the natural order of things. That it's just the way things are, the way things are meant to be, and you need to just suck it up buttercup.

But I want to change that. I want you to see there is another way. I want this book to reignite that flame of desire inside of you that was snuffed out by the lethargy experienced when you spend your life going through the motions and living someone else's idea of what your life should be.

This book is inspired by everyone who decided to take back control and live life on their own terms. By the end of this book, my wish is that you become a member of that illustrious crowd.

INTRODUCTION
LETHARGY TO LIT!

Every day I sit here, I feel like my soul is being sucked out of me.

I would often say this to a colleague during my last couple of years in BigLaw.

To anyone looking at my life from the outside back then, I was living the dream. Here I was, a man from a council estate in Nottingham, England, whose dreams of pop stardom hadn't worked out the way he'd hoped they would. Who'd failed numerous exams, been fired a couple of times and dropped out of university because he didn't see the point. A man who had once been so broke he walked the streets of London in the pouring rain searching for an ATM that would dispense the five

British pounds he needed to pay rent that night. That man had flipped the script and ended up as a BigLaw lawyer at an international law firm with his own office in a building that boasted enviable views across Singapore's Marina Bay.

For the uninitiated, *BigLaw* is a term used to describe the largest, most successful law firms in the world. The firms that take up residence in tall towers of glass and steel. The firms that have offices in multiple jurisdictions housing thousands of highly qualified, super talented lawyers. The term BigLaw relates as much to the financial size of a firm as it does to its physical size. It relates to a certain type of culture, an attitude, a traditional way of doing things. A typical lawyer in BigLaw works long hours in exchange for a high salary and the hope that one day they'll join the illustrious ranks of the partnership and reap the financial rewards and personal prestige such an honour can bring.

That's the glossy picture postcard version.

But if you scratch away the glossy veneer, you'll find a version of BigLaw that doesn't appear in any marketing brochure. A world where for that high salary you're expected to kiss goodbye to any control over your personal time. A world where holidays and weekends can be, and often are, cancelled or interrupted at a moment's notice. A world where sleeping with your phone under your pillow so you don't miss an email isn't an exception but the norm. A world where your needs are secondary to the needs and wants of the firm. A world where you're viewed as a resource whose worth is judged by how many hours you billed that week. A world where if you're told to 'jump', the only acceptable response is to ask, 'How high and what matter should I charge that to?'

I share this to paint a picture of the world I was living in when I was making that dramatic opening statement. I could share more about the darker side of the BigLaw machine, but that would be a whole other book in itself.

Anyway, back to my soul-sucking existence. I'd arrive at the office each day, coffee in hand, rap music blasting through my headphones as I attempted to psyche myself up for another day of lawyering. Once the coffee and the musical high had worn off, I'd struggle to summon the energy and enthusiasm to get even the simplest of tasks done. Then I'd fall into a pit of self-loathing as I berated myself for continuously feeling like I was lazy.

But what I know now that I didn't know then is that I wasn't suffering from laziness; I was suffering from something far worse. I was suffering from lethargy.

What's the difference?

Well, laziness is an unwillingness to do something. Lethargy is a lack of enthusiasm to do something.

Laziness is a character trait. Lethargy is a symptom of feeling unfulfilled, unmotivated, and uninspired.

The two are not the same!

I'm sure you've had days where you've felt that way, right? It's natural; the odd bout of lethargy is to be expected. But when those days turn into weeks, months, or even years of feeling like you're wading through quicksand trying to keep your head up while at the same time thinking, *What's the point?* you've got to ask yourself:

Is this really what I want?

Is this all my life is destined to be?

Do I want to continue living this life of lethargy?

Or do I want to live a life of excitement, joy and purpose – a life that's Lit!?

You're taking the time to pick up and read this book, so I'm guessing the answer is the latter. And, despite everything you may have been told and led to believe by societal expectations, you can have that life. Times have changed. You don't have to 'suck up' a life of lethargy. You don't have to chip away doing something that drains your creativity and kills your energy. Something that makes you consistently feel like a stressed-out cog in a corporate wheel.

See, despite what you've been told, you have a choice.

Yes, you really do.

You can change anything and everything about your situation if you want to.

You can shake things up.

You can flip the script.

You can change course and do something you want to do, instead of silently dying inside doing something you think you should do.

That's why I wrote this book.

Because for a long time, I didn't believe I had a choice. And if I had believed, truly believed, that leaving a 'successful' law career and pursuing an alternative life, a life I wanted, was possible for me, I would have skipped happily away from the fortress of glass and steel that was my office a hell of a lot sooner and saved myself a whole lot of frustration and soul sucking!

I was living a life of lethargy and I didn't even know it. But that lethargy didn't set in overnight. It was built up over years. Years of feeling that being a BigLaw lawyer wasn't working for me. I felt trapped, confined to a way of being that wasn't in line with who I truly was – a free-spirited creative with an aversion to authority.

Do you ever hear a nagging voice in your head questioning your choices? Asking you if you're sure you want to do what you're doing. Asking you if this is it from now until your last breath.

I heard that voice inside my head for five years.

But I ignored it.

Why? Because when you've worked so hard and invested so much time, money and energy into achieving 'success', how do you walk away from that?

When you have a family to take care of and a desire for the finer things in life, you have to just suck it up, right?

After all, isn't that what everyone else does? Complaining about how they hate their job and wish they were doing something else, then coming back to the office day in, day out, year in, year out, surviving, but in no way thriving.

Maybe this is you?

And you know what, it's not your fault. I mean it's true that – and this might be difficult for you to hear – only *you* have the power to change things, so the fact that nothing's changed is ultimately down to you.

But what isn't your fault is that you bought into the lie that we've all been sold. That good grades, a successful corporate job, and a big house with a couple of shiny new cars in the driveway is what success is all about (and in this context, success means high salary and high status). That for you, the average person down the street, toiling away in a gleaming glass and steel cage in exchange for that regular pay cheque and hoping for a decent retirement fund at the end of it all is the only way to live.

Well, guess what, that's all BS!

Like so much of what you've been told is true, you've been sold a lie, a myth. And this book is here to help you dispel that myth and think for and about yourself. The safety and security of corporate life is, and I don't know another way to say this, bollocks!

Throughout history, recession after recession has seen people in so-called 'safe' recession-proof jobs discarded by companies at the first sign of distress to protect their bottom line. And the global pandemic of 2020 has continued this trend in showing us that nothing is certain. The narrative that a corporate role is more secure than entrepreneurship has been ripped apart by numerous people leaving the corporate rat race and setting up their own successful businesses, and the people who started them are now in control of their own fate in a way they never were in the corporate roles that kicked them to the curb when the going got tough.

But I'm running ahead of myself here. When I was where you are now, feeling like I was sinking in quicksand and not knowing how to get out, starting a business seemed crazy! Sure, I had dreams of being a successful entrepreneur, but I never believed I could actually become one.

The voice of my inner critic would ring in my ears saying things like:

People like you don't start businesses.

You can't give up a secure career to chase a dream.

Stay in your lane!

Once a lawyer, always a lawyer.

Until one day I realised I had a choice. That realisation began a shift in how I viewed myself and a belief that I could escape the life of lethargy I felt trapped in. And that belief led me to where I am today, doing things the way I want to do them that aligns with my values, that allows me to express myself fully. I no longer feel the need to squeeze into a box that wasn't designed for me or to do what I think I should do rather than what I want to do.

This feeling, this way of living, is what I call living a life that's Lit! A life where you feel you are living the way you want to live. A life where moments of unbridled excitement, freedom and joy are the norm, rather than the exception. A life where you wake up each morning excited by the possibilities of the day ahead and the opportunity to further your mission. A life of meaning and purpose.

And if you're reading this book, I'm guessing you want this too. And I want to congratulate you on taking the first step to shaking things up and planning your escape from a life of lethargy.

I said it at the start of this chapter, but it needs emphasising: YOU ARE NOT LAZY!

The reason you're going through the motions, feeling unmotivated, unhappy and unfulfilled is because you believe there has to be more. But you don't know what more looks like for you and you can't see a way out of your current situation.

Well, I want you to know, I've got you.

I know change can be overwhelming.

I used to get so overwhelmed sometimes that I'd end up taking the easiest option, which was staying where I was and doing nothing even though I knew the situation wasn't serving me.

But what I've discovered is that you can reduce the overwhelm and start moving forward by focusing on the three Cs that make up The Triple C Method® . These three Cs underpin the work I did on myself to get from where I was to where I am now, and they are the foundation of the work I do with my coaching clients.

What are the three Cs? I'm glad you asked; otherwise, this would be a pretty pointless book! The three Cs are Clarity, Confidence and Courage.

In this book, through sharing my experiences, I'll explain what each C is, why you need it, and how you can get it so that you can move from a life of lethargy to a life that's Lit!

PART 1
CLARITY

DO YOU WANT TO GO
WHERE YOU'RE GOING?

Your gut is your inner compass. Whenever you
have to consult with other people for an answer,
you're headed in the wrong direction.

– Oprah Winfrey

Years ago, a friend and I got on the wrong train.

We were old friends from secondary school. We'd
dated for a while when I was sixteen and had kept in
touch, even though I'd left the city of Nottingham where
we'd met and moved to Sheffield. We hadn't seen each
other in a while, and you know how it is when you catch
up with an old friend; it's like you were never apart. You
pick up exactly where you left off, whether it's been a
day, a week, or a year since you last spoke. I'd travelled
down to Nottingham, from Sheffield, to meet her. And
to add a touch of adventure to proceedings, we figured
it would be fun to head to a neutral city for lunch, rather
than scope out our old familiar haunts. So we headed

to the train station, talking all the way, only stopping to buy our tickets to Leicester and figure out the way to the correct platform. A train rolled into the station at around the time we were expecting ours to arrive and, locked deep in conversation, we got on it.

We sat down, the doors closed, and the train started to pull away from the station. And as is common on trains in the UK, the driver welcomed everyone to the train and started listing the destinations where the train was heading. Fortunately, at that point we'd stopped talking long enough to listen. Unfortunately, the train wasn't heading to Leicester … it was heading to Coventry.

We were on the wrong train!

Doh!

We laughed! I mean, it was inconvenient as it meant we wouldn't get where we were going until much later, but we'd been so engrossed in our own conversation, so cocooned in our own little world, that we would have been happy anywhere.

We managed to get off the train at the next station and we waited for another one to take us back to our original location where we could then start our trip again. But if we hadn't heard that announcement, who knows how long it would have taken us to figure out we were heading to the wrong city.

I tell this story to illustrate how easy it is to get caught up, to drift along without taking the time to question whether you're heading to the right destination.

And keeping that in mind, I'd like you to apply this story to your own life. Think of the train as your career. You likely got on your career train because everyone told you the same old story: go to school, get good grades, go to college or university, start a job at a top law firm or large corporation, and work your way up the ladder. That's life. That's success.

And you did that. You had different ideas and bigger dreams, but you were told they weren't realistic so many times that you believed it. So you did the right thing, obeyed the rules and got on the train without seriously questioning whether it was the right train for you. You followed the crowd. And as you saw everyone else rushing for the same train, you figured you must be heading in the right direction. Maybe for you this was becoming a partner in a law or accountancy firm, a director at a bank, or heading up a department at a major corporation.

But as the years have passed, you've slowly come to realise that you don't want to go where this particular train is heading. So you stand up and look around the carriage, searching for other people who think the same as you, trying to catch someone's eyes to validate your fears. But you notice everyone else is sitting comfortably. You sit back down thinking you must be wrong, so you should suck it up and stay on the train.

Month after month, year after year, you do the stand-up sit-down dance. And each time you do it, the thought of sitting back down and continuing your journey towards a place you don't want to go makes you feel unhappy, unfulfilled, unenthused, stressed, and anxious. But as you can't see an alternative, as you don't have clarity on where you'd like to go instead, you see no option but to keep going, no matter how miserable it makes you to sit at your desk day after day working on matters of no interest, trekking from pointless meeting to pointless meeting, knowing the plans you made weeks ago are about to be destroyed by the 'urgent' deal that's landed on your desk even though you know from experience that the unrealistic deadline won't be met and no one will care.

Does this sound familiar?

Well, this was my story. For five long years, I sat on the BigLaw train, wanting to get off but not having a clue where I would go instead.

Then one day I woke up and realised the train had travelled so far away from where I wanted to be that I was even more lost than I'd been when I first realised. If only I'd trusted my gut and got off the damn train when I first thought about it!

But here's the thing. Without clarity, direction and purpose, getting off the train would have been futile. Changing my external surroundings without doing the inner work to figure out what I really wanted would only have left me in a new environment with the same old feelings.

Gaining clarity was the key that finally led me to stand up on the train one last time, and instead of looking around for validation or support, I opened the door and got off the train.

So what's clarity?

Clarity is defined as 'clearness or lucidity as to perception or understanding'.[1]

I love dictionary definitions. You'll see me use them throughout this book. I love them because they set a foundation of understanding for words that sometimes lose their true meaning from overuse. Dictionary definitions bring us all to the same starting point from which we can begin our journey of exploration, self-inquiry, and self-discovery.

---

1   Dictionary.com, 'Clarity', *Dictionary.com*,
https://www.dictionary.com/browse/clarity, accessed 1 Feb. 2022.

But definitions don't tell the whole story. I mean, yes, clarity is the ability to think about or understand something clearly, but understand what?

I like to use definitions because I take great pleasure in deconstructing them and taking them apart. Kind of like how my two kids like to dismantle their toys! Like father, like sons!

See, when I talk about clarity, I like to take a more expansive view. I'm talking about clarity as to:

- ☑ who you are
- ☑ where you are
- ☑ what you want
- ☑ where you want to be.

That's the level of clarity I'm talking about, and ultimately, although they don't always know this at the outset, this is the clarity my coaching clients need before they can start creating the life they want – a life that's Lit!

We get deeper than this in coaching sessions, but even if you never ever work with a coach, you need to know the answers to these four questions. They seem easy on the surface, but I guarantee when you sit down and really think about them, a whole world of crap will come up that you never thought about. And if you don't do the work to figure this out, well, you'll continue drifting through life without purpose. And this leaves you exposed and at the mercy of other people's opinions, needs and agendas. Why does that matter? Because without knowing the answers, you have no foundation, no anchor point, no North Star to keep you focused on what's important to you.

What do I mean by that?

Well, imagine you've been feeling restless for a while, like something's just not right, so you hire a coach and get answers to the four questions. The answers reveal that you value family and freedom above status and money. Once you know this, you can stop making decisions on the basis that *If I do this, it'll be good for my promotion prospects* because you'll know that sacrificing time with your family and losing more of your freedom to get that promotion isn't in alignment with your values. It's not even a conversation; you know you don't want it, so you can stop stressing over it and stop playing the political game in the hope that one day you'll move up to the next rung on the ladder.

See, clarity makes decision-making easy!

So let's break each of these questions down and get the old grey matter working. You'll also find these questions in the workbook.[2]

---

2   Visit iamryanspence.com/the-triple-c-method-book

Who Are You?

Who are you? Yes, I know, it sounds like a stupid question, but stick with me.

You probably believe that you are who you want to be. That everything you've done and continue to do, and the choices you've made and continue to make, are the result of absolute free will and are determined exclusively by your thoughts.

But have you ever taken the time to think about whether that's actually true?

How much of who you are is influenced by your upbringing?

How much is influenced by your friends?

How much is influenced by what you read, what you watch, or what you listen to?

There's nothing wrong with any of that. It's human nature to be influenced by your surroundings and the people you surround yourself with. But if you don't know the answers to these questions, if you can't separate your actual beliefs from what you've been led to believe, how can you know who you truly are and what you really stand for?

Knowing who you are means knowing what you value. It means knowing what lines you won't cross. It means knowing what you will do and what you won't do, no matter the situation and no matter who may or may not be watching

It means more than the company you work for, the money you make, or the title you hold. You know, the standard responses to most questions asked at corporate networking events.

And believe me when I say it can be uncomfortable doing the work to find out. It can be challenging to discover that the person you thought you were all these years – who wanted to climb the corporate ladder and collect the obligatory status symbols along the way – is not who you really are. It's even more disconcerting when you find out that the things you thought were important, you actually don't give a fuck about. I mean, if your identity is tied to being a lawyer, a banker, an accountant, or a head of sales or operations and what that says about you to people, what happens when you realise that identity isn't yours and never was, that it belongs to someone else!

OK, I might have painted a slightly scary picture here. It's based on my own experience of questioning who I was without the title, the salary and the business card (which until recently, my mother still had in her purse! She was so proud).

But it's all good. Because once you know who you are, you can start to make decisions that align with the real you. You can start to take control of how you're living and where you're heading instead of feeling the need to follow the crowd. And look, you'll get no judgement from me; I've been there.

When you're clear on who you are, what lights you up, and what makes you tick, you're in a position to plan your route towards living the life you want, not the life you think you *should* want.

Got it? OK, next question.

Where Are You?

Now you need to ask yourself 'Where am I?' So, in the most literal sense, you're here reading this book, but you know that's not what I mean!

What I'm asking is:

Where are you in your life right now?

Are you happy? Are you content?

Do you wake up each day with a purpose, a mission that you're working towards? And if so, are you clear on what that mission is? Have you written it down some-where? Do you refer to it often to remind you of why you do what you do?

What about your relationships? Are they all that you wish they could be? Are they loving, fulfilling, supportive?

I know, there are a lot of questions there, right?

But I bet they're questions you've never asked yourself before. And yet, these questions, and the answers to them, are important if you're ever going to experience a life that's Lit! Hands up if you breezed through them, certain that you knew the answers?

I know you did because I've done it myself. Many times. It seems simple, right? Ask a question; give an answer. But unless you've done this work before. Unless you've sat alone with your thoughts and looked deep inside your soul, the answers you came up with as you skipped through my beautifully crafted sections above are, how can I say it, superficial! They have no depth. They're coming from the top of your head – from your conditioned mind that is carrying the baggage of your social conditioning with all the 'shoulds' and limiting beliefs that go along with that.

From my own experience and the experience of working with my clients, once you're forced to sit with your thoughts and really think about them, the true answers take more time to appear than first imagined.

You may also find that when placed under a microscope, the things you thought were working in your life are not actually the things you want! See, just because something is comfortable, it doesn't mean it's the right thing for you. That's how people end up in jobs for years that they're good at, but they feel unfulfilled as each day they're going through the motions, never stepping outside of their comfort zone. But when you're crystal clear on what you want, you'll make the difficult choices, the uncomfortable choices, to get it!

This was the case for one of my clients; let's call her Jasmine.[3] Jasmine was killing it in her career. She'd been headhunted for her most recent job, and all signs pointed to a bright future ahead at the company that hired her. But when she came to me, she was questioning whether she wanted to do what she was doing for the foreseeable future. She wasn't unhappy, but she knew that what she was doing didn't light her up and wanted to explore why that was and what the answer was.

So we started by drilling down into what Jasmine wanted out of life. We worked through what excited her. We dived deep into what her values were. We looked into what she liked and didn't like about her current lifestyle. And we explored the vision of what her ideal life would look like. And through our work together, she realised she was in the wrong place.

One of the key things she valued was family. Having a family of her own one day was important to her. Doing work that was meaningful to her, something that didn't

---

3 Name has been changed.

just involve making more money for people and companies that, quite frankly, don't need more money, was important to her.

And once she visualised what was possible for her and compared it to what her life would look like if she continued living her current life, she decided that the only way to stay true to herself and have any chance of living the life she wanted to live was to quit her job. So that's what she did!

The thing is, she didn't have to. She was fantastic at her job. She didn't hate it. She had a great standard of living by anyone's standard, a promising career, and from the outside looking in, she was successful. But by taking the time to dive deeper, to get clarity on who she was and what she wanted, that self-awareness made her realise that where she was wasn't where she wanted to be, no matter how successful her life looked from the outside.

Where Do You Want to Be?

So, here's where you stand now:

- ☑ You've figured out who you are, and you're not the person you believed you were, and
- ☑ You've figured out where you are, and it's not where you want to be.

The logical next question is, where do you want to be?

I want to be on an island where the sun shines and living is easy (I hate the cold!), but I don't just mean where do you want to be physically.

What does your ideal life – a life that's Lit! – look like for you? And in thinking about this, don't limit yourself. Don't allow ideas of what is and is not realistic hold you back from going all out in creating and visualising your dream life. Because what's realistic is whatever you make real. The power is yours. Sure, it's nice if other people believe in and support your vision, but it doesn't matter if they don't. It's your vision! They're not you and they can't see what you can see.

Maybe your ideal life sees you working from a coffee shop on the beach every day. Where is that beach? Visualise the view, imagine the smell, the sun on your skin; how does it feel?

What's the structure of your day? Does it even have structure, or are you a free-spirited creative type?

I bet you're thinking, *Ryan, you're selling me a pipe dream here.* That's OK. It takes time to start believing that the vision you create in your mind is possible for you. That's why it's important to do the work consistently so that you build up the belief (more on that in the next chapter).

But start small. As you go through your day, notice moments of joy, moments where life feels Lit! It could be that first sip of coffee in the morning. Or your child snuggling into bed with you. Or driving your car with the windows down, Jay Z pumping out loud from your speakers as you rap along to the lyrics like you're on stage at Madison Square Garden ... (Maybe that's just me.)

But notice how you feel in those moments. Then start thinking about what you could do and what you would want to do to make that feeling the norm rather than the exception.

Clarity is key! You owe it to yourself to take the time to get really clear on who you are, what you want, and where you want to be. Without that clarity, you're not living. Instead, like so many people, you're drifting aimlessly through life without direction, without purpose, without a mission. Do you want to be one of those people? I'm guessing the answer is no. So start doing the work now! I'm rooting for you.

KNOW WHAT,
KNOW WHY

The first step is clearly defining what it is
you're after, because without knowing that,
you'll never get it.

– Halle Berry

So you've read chapter 1 and you know what clarity is,
but I want to dive a little deeper into why you need it.

Let me start with taking you through an average day
during my last few years in BigLaw.

Wake up late after snoozing the alarm. Stumble out
of bed bleary-eyed, shower, get dressed and rush out
the door. Grab a coffee (a long black on weekdays and a
mocha on Fridays) and a breakfast bagel of egg, cheese,
bacon and ketchup (back when I still ate animals) on
the way to the office. Sit at my desk, do what I need to
do, all the while feeling progressively more lethargic as
I literally feel the life being sucked out of me. If I managed to escape at a reasonable hour, maybe head for

post-work drinks to blow off some steam and shovel unhealthy bar snacks in my face to help slow down the road to drunkenness. Cab home, feel too wired to sleep, aimlessly scroll through YouTube or Netflix, fall asleep on the sofa, then drag myself to bed asking myself why I always do this to myself. Repeat!

No plan.

No intention.

No sense of achievement (well, maybe surviving the day).

It was pure lethargy as I went through the motions, falling on comfortable old habits to help me through a life unfulfilled.

Sound familiar?

Now, days like this aren't necessarily bad. But when these days become the norm rather than the exception, that's a problem.

OK, now contrast this with what happens when you're clear on what you want, when you're clear on what you're trying to achieve, or when you have a plan or a purpose.

To help you, let me share a story all about how my life got flipped (from a Netflix-bingeing night owl) turned upside down (to a dynamic, energetic early bird).

If you've heard any podcast interview with me, you'll know that it was during a Christmas holiday to Bali in

2018 that I decided enough was enough and I had to figure out a way to escape BigLaw.

I was deep in a funk, my head was foggy, and lethargy had well and truly set in, so I started 2019 determined to shake it off. I needed to get my mind and body in a state from which I would start making some difficult decisions about what I wanted my life to be.

I could have simply hit the gym with all the New Year, New Me folk, done a few classes, and lifted a few weights, but I'd been there and done that and knew that would get pretty old pretty quickly.

No, I needed to do something bold! Something so far outside of my comfort zone that when I told people, they would be like, WTF? Something that would be a complete shock to my lethargic system. Like when your computer freezes and the advice from IT is to turn it off and turn it on again. That's what I needed to do – a hard reboot of my operating system.

Aimlessly googling one quiet Friday afternoon in the office, I saw that applications were open for a charity white-collar boxing match taking place in Singapore that April. I'd done a little boxing on before for fitness and enjoyed the feeling of stress leaving your body as you hit a bag really, really hard, so without really thinking it all through, I found myself submitting my application.

A few days later, I got invited to a briefing about the event. And as I sat through the briefing at the Penny Black pub on Boat Quay in Singapore, I realised the enormity of what I'd signed up for. As I looked around at the other guys in attendance, it dawned on me that I'd be getting in the ring with one of them and opening myself up to being punched in the face in front of one thousand people on fight night.

But I consoled myself with the fact that loads of people had applied, so I was unlikely to get chosen for the squad.

Then a few days later, I received another email congratulating me on making the squad.

FUCK!

Sure, I could have pulled out at that point. But the thing, for better or worse, is that once I say I'm in, I'm all in. So I had three months to get to a state where I could fight and not completely embarrass myself. *Gulp!* On the plus side, this challenge would definitely give me the hard reboot I'd been looking for ... or kill me.

I'll never forget the first week of training. The training schedule was three times per week. Now I had myself down as pretty fit, so although I figured training would be challenging, I had no doubt I'd get through it OK.

Ha!

It was brutal!

It turns out that training to be a fighter is mentally and physically tough. In fact, it's probably one of the hardest things I've ever done. And by the end of week one, my commitment to going all in was hanging by a thread. I was exhausted, everything hurt, and my brain was freaking out and refusing to cooperate with my body. And that's where my foray into the fight game would have ended if I hadn't connected to a clear reason for carrying on.

I needed a Why. Why did I want to put myself through such a gruelling ordeal?

Well, the first Why was the original reason I'd been looking for a challenge. I needed to escape my life of lethargy. I couldn't face being in the same position, feeling the same way, a year from now. As the saying goes, nothing changes if nothing changes. I needed to change myself before I could move forward, and I knew that by taking on such a mammoth task, I'd never be the same person again.

That Why got me to recommit to the game. And once I was committed, I was all in. I wanted to win!

I knew that, given my first week's performance, sticking to the basic training schedule and only attending the group training sessions wasn't going to cut it. I was nowhere near fighting fit, I had zero boxing skills, my footwork was atrocious, and the thought of getting in the ring for sparring filled me with absolute dread!

As you can see, I was no Ali.

So I swallowed my pride, admitted I couldn't do this alone and hired a trainer. And suddenly I went from training for a couple of hours three times a week to training twice a day six times a week. Yep!? Out of the frying pan into the fire!

But boy, did that give me the hard reboot I was looking for. See, no matter how committed we say we are to an outcome, it's a rare being who will consistently push themselves to their absolute limit to achieve it. And it's also a rare being who will consistently carry an unwavering belief in their ability to achieve what they set out to do. In the beginning, I said I wanted to win the fight, but in actuality, I started out not wanting to lose. The two states of mind are not the same.

Fighting not to lose meant doing what I needed to do to put on a good show or, more likely, not put on a bad show. To be able to go out at night, last the distance, and not get knocked out in front of one thousand people.

But fighting to win? That required pushing myself to the very edge of my limits. We all have a limit in our mind of how much we're capable of, what we're capable of achieving. But that limit is false, like those fake walls criminals have in their offices to hide all their illegal paraphernalia (allegedly!). Left to our own devices, we might, on occasion, reach that limit. We'll feel proud of ourselves for reaching it too, proud of the effort exerted to push ourselves to that point. Ya feel me?

Well, here's the secret ... That's not the limit! The limit, your limit, is far beyond that. And to get to your limit, you have to go through some real pain and discomfort. Symptoms can include nausea, shortness of breath, and an inability to stop swearing!

Now, how likely are you to push yourself that hard when it's just you? With the best will in the world, I'd say pretty unlikely. That's why even the best athletes in the world have coaches. To push them when they don't feel like it. To get them to their limit when they feel like quitting. And to see the vision for them that they can't see for themselves amidst the pain and discomfort.

So, after that dismal first week, I got clear on my Why and hired a coach to get me there.

Now, the only reason I talk about myself in this book is to paint a picture that you can relate to, so let's bring this back to you, dear reader.

How is a story of my boxing prowess (or lack thereof) relevant to your life?

Well, it illustrates that once you have clarity of your end goal and your Why, you'll start making decisions that support that Why and stop making decisions that don't support it.

Once I was clear on my objective – to win the boxing match – I made decisions to support that objective like giving up alcohol, paying close attention to my diet, not skipping training sessions, and, yes, hiring a coach.

Previously when I headed to the gym or entered a race without a clear objective, I made decisions like trying to out-train a poor diet, treating training sessions as optional rather than mandatory, and saying yes to post-work drinks, which inevitably meant missing the next morning's run or weights session.

I say all this to illustrate that without being clear on your goal, you won't know where you're going, which means you won't know what you're meant to be doing on any given day, which means you'll lack direction, which means you'll waste time procrastinating, over-thinking, scrolling through Instagram or, even worse, being held hostage to someone else's agenda because you have nothing of your own to guide you. The end result is lack of growth and lack of progress.

If you don't have clarity, you're like the person I talked about earlier in this book who gets on the wrong train and stays there because you have no idea what you want or why you're going where you're going.

You're not present. You're on autopilot. You feel lethargic so you fall asleep. Then you wake up wondering where you are and how the hell you got there.

That's why you need clarity.

The thing about clarity, though, is that it's not always obvious that you don't have it. Very meta right – you don't have clarity on your clarity! But it's something I've experienced and that I've seen with clients.

What do I mean?

Well, take BigLaw, for example. In BigLaw, there's a clear road to progression. And knowing this road from the outset provides a degree of clarity as you know the career progression checkpoints along the road. But what happened to me, and what I see happening to many others, is that you're so excited at being accepted into that world that you see the well-mapped-out road ahead of you and don't question whether that's the road you *want* to follow. Instead, you accept it as a clear sign of the road you *must* follow.

It's like the story I shared at the beginning of the previous chapter.

I got on the BigLaw train with excitement at the road ahead, sat down, and passively let the train carry me along. I had thought I wanted to go where the train was heading because that's what everyone around me said I should want, so I thought I should want it too. And in doing that, I didn't check in from time to time to see whether I wanted to go where the train was heading.

I assumed I was heading in the right direction because the train was full and more people were trying to get on the train.

But it was the wrong train for me!

And that's why no matter what you're trying to achieve in life, clarity is key!

Whether you want to:

- ☑ achieve balance
- ☑ increase your productivity
- ☑ eliminate overwhelm
- ☑ find direction and meaning in what you do
- ☑ make more money

Everything starts with clarity.

Conversely, without clarity, you'll spend your time making decisions that don't serve you, reacting to other people's agendas, doing what they want you to do, and going where they want you to go.

And look, I know as well as anyone that it's not easy to find clarity amongst the chaos and distractions of life. Even when I began my personal development quest in 2019, I found it hard to sit and do the deep work necessary to answer the questions I pose in this book. That lack of direction resulted in multiple half-read books and hours spent down YouTube rabbit holes and drowning in Google searches, as I got distracted by the next shiny idea or strategy.

I swear if I hadn't invested in myself and hired a coach, I'd probably still be trapped down one of those rabbit holes or still drifting along a road I didn't want to be on, which would have been a tragedy because you would never have got to read this book.

So tempting as it might be to skip the uncomfortable stuff, I urge you to pause. Take a breath. And focus on getting clarity. Answer the questions in the workbook and you'll have your own GPS to guide you towards the life you want.

3

DON'T THINK ABOUT IT;
BE ABOUT IT

Don't sit down and wait for the opportunities
to come. Get up and make them.

– Madam C.J. Walker

So now that you know what clarity is and why you need
it, I guess you're wondering how you get it?

One word. Action!

When you take action, everything becomes clearer.
You need to try things and get out of your head to see
what works for you and what can be left behind. *Action*
means doing something for a particular purpose[4]. That
doesn't mean constant physical movement; it means
being intentional, and the first step in gaining clarity is
arguably the hardest – doing the inner work to get to the
essence of who you are.

---

4   Collins Dictionary, 'Action' https://www.collinsdictionary.com/
dictionary/english/action accessed 5 Feb 2022.

The inner work is uncomfortable. Sitting alone with your thoughts can uncover stories and truths that you thought were long forgotten. But every story and every truth has forged your outlook and personality, and they have carved out your habits and thought patterns. If you start rushing ahead, trying all the things without uncovering these truths and understanding these stories, it will be as if you're driving under the influence – you won't be in control.

You need to unpick the stories, figure out what serves you without judgement, and let the rest go. It's akin to shedding layers of yourself that have been built up to protect you until you get to the absolute essence of who you are without the armour you've been carrying around to keep you safe and comfortable.

The inner work can be complex and messy, and there may be a lot of ugly crying along the way, but it's necessary if you're to have any chance of living life Lit! You can start by asking yourself the questions in chapter 1, which I helpfully recap and expand on later in this chapter. We don't take enough time to sit and ask ourselves these questions. I get it, life's busy, and we're conditioned to avoid discomfort.

But these questions are important to making a shift, to making a real change. And I've found carving time out of your week to reflect on them is one of the most valuable things you can do to get the clarity you need to change your mindset and ultimately change your life. That's where journaling comes in. You spend hours each week investing in your job, why not take some time to invest in yourself? The return on investment will be a whole lot greater.

Now, I know you've heard many people recommend journaling, but before you dismiss what I'm about to say, hear me out. I'm not going to tell you to get up at 5 a.m. and spend an hour journaling every day while inhaling the aroma of luxury coffee made from beans handpicked from cat poo! Yes, this is a real thing, but please don't do it.[5]

I don't journal consistently. I know, shock, horror, a coach who doesn't journal!

Well, that's not strictly true. When I say I don't journal consistently, what I mean is I don't have a journaling routine. I don't sit down at the same time every day and diligently write down my thoughts in beautiful cursive script. But when I do journal, I find that the floodgates

---

5   Priya S, 'Civet Coffee – a Sip of Cruelty', PETA UK (30 Sept. 2019), https://www.peta.org.uk/blog/civet-coffee-a-sip-of-cruelty, accessed 1 Feb. 2022. Kopi luwak is made from beans of coffee berries eaten and excreted by the Asian palm civet. The production of this coffee has been described by PETA as cruel and the sale of it, repugnant.

open and everything gushes out of my head onto paper in an uncontrollable flow, and it's a powerful feeling.

We edit ourselves so much in life that allowing ourselves to let everything out in a stream of consciousness without judgement is a liberating experience. If you've ever had resistance towards journaling, think of it as emptying the trash in your mind. You wouldn't let your bins at home overflow without emptying them, so why would you do that to your most valuable asset, your mind?

To help you with the mental trash dumping, I invite you to ask yourself the following three questions. They're questions I ask my clients and I revisit them personally from time to time as I enter a higher level of growth. There's a headline question followed by a number of sub-questions to encourage you to go deeper and break through any resistance.

Who Are You?

Who are you sounds like a simple question, right? Almost laughable in its simplicity. But that's because you need to go deeper than surface level and ask, really, *Who am I? Who am I deep within my soul, without the crutch of my career status? What are my values? What excites me? What lights me up? What fulfils me?*

It takes time to get to the answers. It takes a willingness to confront and question all that you believe to be true and be open to the fact that those beliefs may not be your own – accepting that those beliefs may be a construct of parental and societal conditioning masquerading as the real you. But you can't move forward without first doing the work and sitting with the thoughts and emotions that arise on your way to the answer. And as you grow, as circumstances change, that answer may change. Allow that. Don't fight it. Evolution leads to greater knowledge of self, so keep checking in with yourself as each shift happens. Who are you at that particular moment?

Let's move on to the next question.

What Do You Want?

What do you want out of life? Do you want the freedom to live and work wherever you want? Do you want to have a family? Do you want an ordinary life or an extraordinary life? Do you want security above all else? Do you want to be an entrepreneur with all the emotional ups and downs that come with it? Maybe you crave the quiet life, and your idea of heaven is spending your days sitting on the dock of the bay watching the tide roll away.

Whatever it is, the emphasis is on you. What do *you* want? What's *your* dream? We're all influenced more than we believe by what everyone else thinks we should want or by what society says we should want. You know, the whole traditional path of getting good grades, getting a good job, and rising up the corporate ladder.

But have you ever taken the time to ask yourself if that's what *you* want? Have you used your critical thinking muscle (as my coach, Ruby, would say) to question that? Have you actually thought about whether that life is the life for you? Let your mind run free here and don't hold back from writing down everything you want, yes, even the things you think you might be judged or ridiculed for like 'I want to be a bestselling author' or 'I want to win the Nobel Peace Prize.'

And when you've figured out what you want, the final question is:

Why Do You Want It?

Why do you want this thing? What is it about the thing or things you want that would make you happy? What is it about it or them that excites you? Autonomy is a key value of mine. The ability to live and work anywhere, have complete control of my day, and be able to decide who I work with, when I work with them, where I work with them, and how I work with them. That's one of the things I want. It's extremely important to me.

Why?

Because I want to work with people who are doing things that excite me, but also doing things that excite them, that are going to help them and the people around them. I want to be around people who have or are trying to find a mission, and I want to help them make huge breakthroughs and transformations as they strive towards fulfilling that mission. Because seeing people striving to reach their full potential come through the other side and realise that potential lights me up. It excites me.

I want to be able to take off with my kids whenever I want, head to the cinema in the middle of the day or head off on holiday and not have to worry about whether my annual leave application will be approved or not. Ultimately, I want that feeling of waking up knowing that I can do anything I want to do that day.

Knowing that these things drive me allows me to make intentional decisions that align with what I want.

So now you see how intentionally taking action to regularly reflect on these three questions will help you develop clarity. And with that clarity, you can begin to live in a way that aligns with who you are, what you want, and why you want it. Clarity allows you to be more discerning in your decisions. To easily decide whether or not to do something based on whether it fits in with what you believe and the vision of the life you want.

It stops you from spinning your wheels when you find yourself at a crossroads as you'll instinctively know which way to go. It won't matter where anybody else is going; you'll know with absolute certainty the path to take – the path that will lead you to where you want to be.

Clarity stops you from being distracted by the noise around you and provides a strong foundation for levelling up the next C in the triumvirate, the topic of part 2 of this book, Confidence!

PART 2
CONFIDENCE

IF YOU BELIEVE YOU CAN,
YOU PROBABLY CAN

The first step is you have to say that you can.

– Will Smith

Have you ever believed something so deep in your soul that you can see it? That it's as if you're watching yourself in a movie doing the thing? You don't just believe it with your mind; you believe it with your whole being; you feel that rush of adrenaline, fast-beating heart, and immense power flow through your body as you visualise yourself in the perfect place, at the perfect time, doing the perfect thing.

And at that moment, any resistance you may have felt melts away as you step up to do the thing you know you were born to do?

Just writing that brought me out in all the feels. What image was painted in your mind as you read that?

For me, it took me back to being on stage and my dream of being a pop star.

I always performed as a child. I was introspective, a little awkward sometimes, and I didn't always fit in, but every time I got on stage, I felt at home.

My earliest memory of public performance is standing behind a lectern at primary school. I must have been about eight years old, wearing a bright red velvet cape as I narrated that year's nativity play (I may have been awkward, but I could be pretty badass at times). I absolutely loved it! I was immediately hooked on the feeling of being the centre of attention and having the audience hang on my every word. This became an ongoing theme throughout my school life and beyond, often to the detriment of what I should have been focusing on, like schoolwork, for instance!

From that first moment, deep in my soul, I knew that I wanted to be a performer. In fact, I'd go further than that and say I knew without a shadow of a doubt that my life would involve being on stages around the world. I didn't know how I was going to get there, and I didn't need to because I had such an innate belief in my ability to perform and 'sell out' shows.

So how does an eight-year-old child acquire such unwavering confidence?

It came from a will to do the thing I loved. It came from a willingness to devote hours to practising singing and dancing. It came from saying yes to any opportunity I got to perform both for the joy of performing and in the hope that I'd be seen by someone who could help make my dream a reality.

Weirdly, when I was off stage, I wasn't confident at all, but on it with the lights down and all eyes on me, my belief in my ability to rock a crowd was unwavering.

For years I carried the desire for superstardom and had the utmost confidence in my ability to be a successful recording artist. That desire carried me through failed exam after failed exam as I placed all my focus on achieving my dream and very little on achieving good grades.

In my mind, I didn't need good grades. My calling was the stage, and I didn't need school for that. Even when I finally went back to Sixth form college and got the grades to go to university, my dream of pop stardom remained alive. I chose my university, Buckinghamshire Chilterns University College in High Wycombe, based on its proximity to London, the music capital of the UK, and some might say the world. I spent my entire first year travelling back and forth to London, a forty-minute train ride away, trying to break into the music industry, leading to, you guessed it, failed exam after failed exam.

I managed to scrape through to year two, but it was only a matter of time before I dropped out to work for a record company and began managing and writing for a couple of new recording artists. By that time, performing was still a thing, but my focus had shifted slightly to being a music mogul like Sean 'Diddy' Combs, who at that time had the Midas touch in terms of creating major R'n'B and hip-hop stars. So the opportunity to focus on music 24/7, live in London, and keep forging ahead towards my ultimate dream was everything I wanted.

Well, almost everything. The slight wrinkle in the whole picture-perfect existence was that I had no money. I was broke. Really broke. I mean negative thousands of pounds broke. I was so broke that when I put my card into the ATM, I saw the words insufficient funds more often than I saw any cash coming out. On more than one occasion, the machine would swallow my card, meaning another embarrassing visit to the bank as I pleaded my case for a new card and another small increase in my overdraft facility. I lived in a shitty room in a shitty flat, which I chose for its proximity to the office so that I didn't have to pay any commuting costs. And that shitty flat, one of the few places I could afford on my meagre income, not only took half my salary but the roof leaked when it rained and more than once we had a rodent problem.

What was mad about the whole thing was that I'd attend star-studded industry parties with free food and free alcohol, then go home on the night bus because there was no way I could afford a cab back to my awful flat with the leaky roof. And as for holidays, forget about it! My holidays were basically work trips where I travelled with the artist I managed to perform at shows in Ibiza, Germany, and Ayia Napa. I describe my life at that point as being both the best of times and the worst of times.[6]

But I absolutely loved what I did, I had complete confidence in my ability, and I knew it was only a matter of time before the rewards I was seeking would materialise.

Then that raging inferno of confidence that burned so brightly for so long started to flicker.

I don't know when it started. Maybe it was when my friends started to leave university and get jobs that paid them what, at the time, seemed to me to be a fortune. Maybe it was when the licensing deal the company I was working for was trying to put together with a bigger record company didn't work out in the way my boss and I had anticipated. Maybe it was the grind of living in London, one of the most expensive cities in the world,

---

6   Paraphrasing a quote made popular by Charles Dickens's book *A Tale of Two Cities*.

and not being able to fully experience all it had to offer as I was perpetually broke!

Whatever it was, that supreme confidence I'd once had was replaced by what I now know were limiting beliefs. And I carried those limiting beliefs with me for many, many years to come, to the point that limiting beliefs held me back from getting after what I wanted. It was limiting beliefs that led to me leaving the music business to become a lawyer. My experience in the music business was that the lawyers always got paid first, so to have any chance of making money in the music business, I needed to become a lawyer. That was a limiting belief.

Does the term limiting beliefs mean anything to you?

If it does, you're already further ahead than I was when I left the music business and, much later, when I first entertained the idea that I needed to escape BigLaw. The term limiting beliefs wasn't something I was familiar with.

I know exactly what they are now though, and what I've learned on my journey from BigLaw lawyer to BigLaw dropout is that limiting beliefs equate to a lack of confidence. Knowing that, and looking back at my time in the music business with the knowledge I have now, explains why self-doubt about my ability to earn a living beyond BigLaw kicked in, my limiting beliefs grew, and my confidence fell. Why the self-doubt? Because the memory of being broke in my music business days never left me and I feared going back. And because I had no relatable blueprint for someone like me who had given up a successful legal career and used their own creativity to make money and become successful in a different field.

Continuing with my love of dictionary definitions, *Confidence* is defined as 'the quality of being certain in your abilities or of having trust in people, places, or the future'.[7] It's a belief in your ability to do or achieve something. It's also a belief in your ability to figure things out. Conversely, a lack of confidence is a lack of belief.

And that lack of belief, or lack of confidence, shows up in the stories you tell yourself.

Need some examples?

OK, I got you!

When you say to yourself things like:

☑ *I'll never be able to do that; I don't have [fill in the blank].*

☑ *It's impossible to change course now. I just have to suck it up.*

☑ *That's for other people, not people like me.*

---

7   Cambridge Dictionary, 'Confidence', *Cambridge Advanced Learner's Dictionary*, https://dictionary.cambridge.org/dictionary/english/confidence, accessed 1 Feb. 2022.

- ☑ *It's all too hard for someone like me.*
- ☑ *I don't like it, but it's just the way things are supposed to be.*

That's your lack of confidence showing up to limit your belief in what you're capable of.

When I realised BigLaw wasn't right for me but still lacked the belief that I could change course and do something different, I was limiting my belief as to what was possible for me.

When I told myself I'd love to start my own business, but I didn't believe I had any viable ideas or that anybody would be interested in what I had to offer, I was limiting my belief as to what was possible for me.

When I decided that entrepreneurship wasn't for 'people like me' and I was destined to continue doing a job I didn't want to do for the rest of my life, I was limiting my belief as to what was possible for me.

And the interesting thing about these stories I was telling myself is that I had absolutely no evidence that those beliefs were true! As a lawyer, you'd think I'd be used to dealing in fact, not fiction, right? (Eye-roll.)

So to repeat, because I don't think this point can be overstated, ***a limiting belief equates to a lack of confidence in your ability to do or achieve something without any evidence to support that belief.*** And your lack of confidence manifests itself in the stories you tell yourself that hold you back from getting after what you want and keep you living in a way you don't want to live.

But before you start beating yourself up about all this, I want you to know that this is all part of being human. These limiting beliefs are the brain's way of keeping you safe, of protecting you from the perceived danger of the unknown.

And as you continue to level up and grow, you'll continue to run into limiting beliefs, which is why it's important to keep doing the inner work, through coaching and therapy, to combat them.

In writing this book, my mind was filled with a truckload of limiting beliefs, and some of them spun me out for a hot minute. But the fact you're reading this book means I did the work to deal with them. And it demonstrates that it's possible for you to deal with yours by developing tools and strategies to take them down when they rear their ugly head.

Don't get it twisted though.

This isn't about 'faking it until you make it'. That's a short-term fix that fails to get to the heart of understanding why you held those limiting beliefs in the first place. It's like sticking a band-aid on an infected wound without cleaning it first. I know, I know, you were reading this while enjoying a nice meal, and now I've put this gruesome image in your head (sorry, not sorry), but I hope it helps you get the picture.

Building confidence is an ongoing process of training your brain to accept that you can do hard things and that you can do anything you put your mind to.

Confidence allows you to think big. It allows your thoughts to expand beyond your previously limited horizon and gives you the belief that everything you dream of is possible for you.

In my case, confidence gave me the belief that I could move beyond BigLaw. It took a lot of work to get to that point. It took self-reflection to help me see when I was presenting limiting beliefs as fact without the evidence to support them. It took self-inquiry, asking myself questions that helped me reframe thoughts so they served me rather than disempowered me.

And by doing this inner work, I built enough confidence to unlock the door of my mental cell, step outside and see a whole world of opportunity before me. It took self-awareness to realise that I was trapped in a mental cell of self-limitation – a cell of my own making that only I could release myself from. It took carving out time to sit with the questions posed in this book and search for the real answers, not simply settle for the easy answers.

I spent years haphazardly reading books, performing Google searches, and watching YouTube videos that took me down rabbit holes, avoiding digging deep into the essence of what I feared and how to overcome those fears.

Nothing changed because I wasn't fully committed to the process. And if you're not committed to something, you get easily distracted by the next shiny object. In my case that meant I jumped from information to information, strategy to strategy, and never focused on following anything through. The word *focus* can be broken down to mean Follow One Course Until Success. Once I started doing that, that focus brought clarity and that clarity lit a fire under me that led to me developing the confidence that I could figure out how to get what I wanted in life. Too many people, including myself, worry about having to know the 'how' before they take action. When you have confidence, you trust that once you know the 'what' you can figure out the 'how' along the way.

Confidence is the quality of being certain in your abilities or of having trust in people, places, or the future. And you're gonna need that confidence if you're going to stand a chance of moving from a life of lethargy to a life that's Lit!

Why do you need it? Read the next chapter to find out!

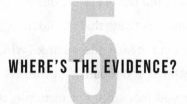

WHERE'S THE EVIDENCE?

> The only thing stopping you from achieving your
> dreams are the stories you keep telling yourself
> that you can't.
>
> – Denzel Washington

Why do you need confidence? Plenty of people say they don't have confidence and they do fine in life. Even outwardly successful people profess that deep down, they're not confident. But nobody lacks confidence; they simply haven't activated the confidence within themselves. It's like when you get a new ATM card from the bank. If you put the card into the machine as soon as you receive it in the mail, it won't work. That doesn't mean you don't have money in your account; it just means you haven't set a new PIN code and activated your card to be able to access those funds. It's the same with confidence. Everyone has a balance in their confidence account, but not everyone has yet figured out the personal code to activate that confidence.

Have you ever heard the saying 'Where attention goes, energy flows'?[8] It means that your energy is drawn to whatever you focus on. For example, if you have a scarcity mindset and focus on having no money, you'll perpetually have no money. If you focus on how bad you are at something, you'll continue to be bad at the thing. If you focus on your inability to do something, chances are you'll never be able to do it. And if your attention drifts away from the thing you were focusing on, your energy flows right along with it, which, as I'll share with you, can lead to almost catastrophic results!

Let me take you back to my music business days for a moment. As I said, I used to manage recording artists. I loved it! Not only did I get to be involved in the creative process of songwriting, song selection, and photoshoots I also got to deal with the business side of negotiating and booking gigs then travelling with the artists to perform at the shows.

This meant late nights cruising up and down the motorways of the UK, sometimes to towns that, even as a born and bred Brit, I'd never heard of before. On the

---

8   Often attributed to James Redfield, an American author and lecturer.

way to the gigs, the car would often have a party atmosphere, music blasting, singalongs by me, the artist, and
whoever was tagging along with us that night; it was a
lot of fun. But heading back from a gig could be a bit of a
downer at times. You know what it's like when you have
an amazing night out then have to make the long trek
home? Yeah, that feeling of coming down from a major
adrenaline high and dealing with the reality of having
to find your way home – that's the post-gig feeling. And
the further away from home the gig was, the more pronounced the downer.

We were returning from a gig in the north of England
one night, heading down the M1 motorway back towards High Wycombe (where I lived) and London
(where the artist lived), and that familiar post-gig feeling kicked in as soon as we hit the motorway. There
were just the two of us in the car on this trip, the artist
and me. I was driving and she quickly fell asleep in the
back of the car within minutes of me guiding the car
onto the motorway.

Driving on a motorway at any time can be boring.
Everything looks the same; there's none of the variety
of scenery that you get when driving through a town or
city, and that boredom is amplified at night when the
roads are quieter, and you're left alone with nothing but
your thoughts.

I was doing what I usually did to stem the boredom, singing along to music, but after a certain point, that just wasn't cutting it, and I felt myself drifting. I opened the car window to let the cool air caress my face in the hope that it would keep me focused and awake, and that worked ... until it didn't!

To this day, I can't remember exactly what I was thinking about. Maybe how the gig went? Or what I had to do the next day? Or how hungry I was? Or why I hadn't gone over and talked to the girl who smiled at me when I walked off stage? Who knows? Anyway, it doesn't matter. What matters, and the reason I'm telling you this story, is that amidst whatever thoughts were drifting around in my head, there came an almighty *Bang!*

For what must have only been a matter of seconds, I had let the boredom, tiredness, and my thoughts get the better of me. My attention had drifted away from the road, and although my hands remained in the same position on the steering wheel, instead of continuing in a straight line I veered off to the right and collided with the central reservation barrier. To say it was scary AF would be an understatement! Aside from the time some idiot crashed into the back of my mum's car when I was younger, I'd never been in a car accident before.

The sleeping singer in the back of the car woke up with a jolt, and my heart dropped all the way down and seemingly out of my body as I felt a cold sweat come over me. Somehow, and I've no idea how. I had managed to restart the car and steer it over towards the hard shoulder before coming to a stop. Getting out to inspect the damage, I saw that the previously white paintwork was now interspersed with the cold silver of bare steel where I'd scraped the entire right side of the car along the safety barrier. Fortunately, given that it was around 2 a.m., there were no other cars around and neither of us was hurt.

That story still gives me the chills when I think about it because if the circumstances were different, it could have ended much, much worse.

I share this story to illustrate what happens when you allow your attention to be taken away from the main thing in front of you, the thing you're trying to achieve. My attention drifted to my random thoughts, and my energy followed, leaving the car to be driven by, effectively, a human shell!

This is also what limiting beliefs do if you let them. They gradually take your attention away from the main thing. Then before you know it, your focus is no longer on the road ahead and you're asleep at the wheel, consumed by your thoughts, driving in a direction you don't want to go in. You keep travelling in that direction until you collide with your own version of the central reservation barrier – maybe a health scare, relationship breakdown, or job loss. And this shocks you back into a state of self-awareness as you attempt to refocus your vision and your mind in the hope that you can still get to where you want to get to despite the time lost and damage caused.

Sure, limiting beliefs are just thoughts, but thoughts are powerful. As my car crash story shows, thoughts have the power to determine your actions. And those thoughts become self-fulfilling prophecies. You think you can't do something; you focus on that thought and it holds you back from doing the thing. The thought stops you from taking action to make that goal a reality, and it keeps you stuck in a place where you don't want to be.

That's why you need confidence. Building and boosting your confidence will help you counteract those limiting beliefs and get you believing in your ability to make shit happen. Confidence shifts your attention from what you can't do to believing you can figure it out. Because confidence generates this belief within yourself that no matter what thoughts might be swirling around in your head, they're just thoughts. Those thoughts are just stories you're telling yourself – stories that have no evidence to back them up. And when you realise that confidence allows you to challenge those thoughts, ultimately you dismiss them from your mind.

If you're reading this and thinking, *But Ryan, I'm not like you, I'm not a confident person.* Let me tell you, the man you see staring out at you from the back of this book was absolutely dripping with self-doubt and low confidence for years! As I said earlier, the only place I felt truly confident was on stage. So trust me when I tell you I don't have some special confidence pill that I take, and I wasn't given an overdose of confidence at birth. It took a lot of work to get to this point, and even with all that work, I still have moments where my confidence levels take a dip, usually when I'm stepping up to do something I haven't done before that's outside my comfort zone. The difference now is that I have the tools and strategies to deal with the thoughts and boost my confidence so I can keep moving forward.

You're not alone in thinking that confidence is something only you struggle with or in staring in awe at the confidence you see some people possess but believe you'll never have. But as I said at the start of this chapter, we all have confidence. Confidence is within you, within me and within every one of us. It's not something that only the privileged few are born with. It's not something that's determined by your wealth or your status. It's something that you cultivate. Like working out in the gym or training for a boxing match, you've got to put in work, practise consistently, and get in those reps to build it.

Without doing that work, without belief in yourself, without confidence, you'll never achieve those audacious goals, and you'll always wonder what might have been if you'd just done the work to believe in yourself. You'll spend your days gazing wistfully at people doing the thing you wanted to do, and you'll lament the fact that you didn't or, in your mind, couldn't do the same, as if it were down to some character flaw that you possessed.

But you're not flawed! You just haven't done enough practice. Trust me, when you do that practice, build that inner belief, and build that confidence, you won't be thinking, *If only I could do that*. No, you'll consider it done! As clearly as you see the words on this page right now, you'll see yourself doing the thing you want to do, having the thing you want to have, and you'll believe it's possible for you. You'll trust and believe that once you know the 'what' and just start getting after what you want, you can figure out the 'how' along the way.

When your thoughts are telling you, *I can't*, confidence will make you ask, *Where's the evidence?* When your brain is telling you, *That's not for me*, confidence will make you ask, *Why not me?*

Have I got you hyped up now? Are you starting to think that maybe there's something to this 'everybody has confidence' thing that this random guy from the UK is telling you? Are you keen to find out how you can get it?

Well, keep reading, my friend. You're in just the right place.

PRACTICE MAKES PROGRESS

Practice creates confidence.
Confidence empowers you.

– Simone Biles

I could see the excitement quickly turn to nervousness as he stepped into his harness and watched the safety briefing. The brightly coloured walls that had looked so appealing from afar now seemed so high and the thought of climbing them was about to become a reality. He looked at me and said 'Daddy, I'm nervous.' My first instinct was to tell him to go ahead, he'd be fine, but instead I gave him the opportunity to change his mind. 'It's fine to be nervous Lukey; what do you want to do?' I could see him thinking through, trying to decide whether he wanted to go ahead with the climb or not. Then he said, 'I want to go climbing, Dada.' And I was the proudest father in the world at that moment!

As the time came for him to make his way to the climbing walls, he looked over at me again with a smile then strode over to the first wall. The attendant hooked him in, Luca looked up, then he started to climb. He took around five steps up then jumped down, allowing the line to gently lower him down to the floor as if he were flying. A grin sprung up across his face. Then he did it again, this time climbing a little higher. Then again, higher, again higher, each time floating down to the ground with the grace of an eagle and sporting a grin like that of a hyena. Now he was in his element. He'd found his groove. He switched from wall to wall and with each climb his confidence grew. For his last few climbs, he picked the tallest wall, and on his first attempt, you could see the hesitation as he tentatively climbed a handful of steps before dropping down. I called him over and said, 'You can do this, Luca. Look at all the other walls you've climbed. This is no different; just do what you were doing before and you'll be fine.' That grin came back and he said, 'OK Dada' before walking back to the wall and scaling it like a pro! As our time slot came to an end, he squeezed in one last climb. And as he floated down for the final time, the grin on his face seemed to be even bigger than those before as he shouted to me, 'Dada, that's the highest I've ever climbed!' Forget what I said earlier, that was my proudest dad moment.

This is the story of my six-year-old son's first time at a climbing wall, and I'm telling you this as it's the perfect illustration of how you get confidence ... practise!

You can't sit around thinking about being more confident and hope that it comes to you. You've got to consistently practise and train your confidence muscle. Confidence is like anything; the more you practise building it, the easier it becomes to tap into that confidence when you need it. It's not about faking it. It's not about bravado. It's not about arrogance. There's a fine line between confidence and each of these things, and you must ensure you're on the right side of that line.

My son was nervous about climbing because he'd never done it before. He didn't know what to do. But he wanted to climb, and after weighing up the options in his mind, he decided to go ahead, try it, and trust he could figure it out. And that's what you need to do. You need to accept you won't be great at everything the first few times and focus on boosting your belief in your ability to figure things out. I know this is hard. When from the outside you appear to be a cool, calm, collected high achiever, but the thought of doing something you're not good at, where you don't yet have proficiency and you don't have a piece of paper certifying your competence, is terrifying. Why? Because you've been wired to believe that the only acceptable standard when doing anything is perfection. The mythical gatekeepers of life have led you to believe that there's a particular way of doing things and that some things are only for some people. But here's what I've learned: perfection is an illusion and there is no 'right way'. So if you're waiting until you're perfect or for someone to give you permission, you'll never start. And if you never start, how will you know what you're capable of? How will you build your confidence?

The idea that you have to be good at something before you can do it is odd if you think about it. Because everything you can do now had to be learned. You had to learn to walk, talk, run, read, play a musical instrument or play a sport. School was one big learning experience; university was another. And as for the world of work, compared to what you know now, you knew absolutely nothing when you started. But look at you now. So with all the evidence you have of learning to do new things, why is it so hard to believe you can't take that same drive and intelligence to learn about something you really want to do?

These words come from a living place of knowing. Because I've been there questioning and doubting to the point of paralysis. Take this book, for instance. As I said in the preface, I always dreamed of writing a book. But I didn't have the confidence to do it until now. The idea of sharing the thoughts in my head, in a book, that anyone could read, was absolutely terrifying! I would look wistfully on as people I admired released books and became authors, and I'd wish I could do that too. So what changed? Confidence. I built confidence in my belief that I could do anything I wanted to do. I built confidence in my belief that there was no evidence in the story I was telling myself that I, Ryan Spence, couldn't write a book. The only evidence was that I hadn't written a book before. So I intentionally set about building trust in my ability to figure out how to do it.

But don't get it twisted. It was still an uncomfortable endeavour. Remember when I said you'll likely be terrible the first time you do something? Well, I recall sitting in a hotel room in Leeds, UK, reading the first draft of this book and being absolutely horrified at how awful it was. Cue all the spinning out in my head. It was like when you pop a pin in a balloon and it flies indiscriminately around the room. That was my confidence deflating into a shrivelled heap on the floor of a room at the Marriott. But after taking some time to sit in the puddle of my metaphorical tears, I told myself the same thing I'm telling you now: everyone's shit at something the first time they do it. It's in the shit that growth happens. That's why farmers spray manure on their crops. Accepting that fact but going for it anyway is the only way to banish your demons and build your confidence. That's the practice. And in telling myself that I could, no, that I had to get back up and start writing again, I rebuilt my confidence to a place where I was able to finish writing the book that you're now holding in your hands.

And my confidence is so high right now that even if you're thinking to yourself, *Well, this book is still shit*, I really don't care.

Joke! (Or is it?) But seriously, that's the energy I want you to take away from reading this. That IDGAF[9] energy. Because once you have that energy, once you have that level of confidence, not a damn thing can hold you back from getting after what you want.

One of the things I wrestled with once I knew I wanted to leave BigLaw was the concept of sunk cost fallacy. The idea that I'd invested so much time, energy and money in getting to where I was, a senior associate in a top ten law firm, that I couldn't possibly walk away from that. In my mind, I had committed myself to forever being a lawyer in a BigLaw practice. And I was good at it. So to give that up to do something else would surely be madness, right?

---

9   I Don't Give A Fuck.

I know now that was my lack of confidence shining through. By that point in my life, I'd managed to navigate a number of different jobs, got myself a first class law degree while working full-time, and secured a job at a top ten law firm despite my unconventional education path that included dropping out of university the first time around! So why the hell did I think I couldn't figure out a path beyond BigLaw?

I didn't see all of that at the time. I was in the thick of things, which meant I couldn't see the wood for the trees. But when I began to commit to my personal growth and development and focus on doing the inner work, this had a positive effect on my confidence, to the point that I realised how lucky I was. I was lucky because I had a choice. I could do anything.

Realising that freed me to make the best decision for me, which was to leave BigLaw. Yes, BigLaw has its problems that are well documented: the hours, the culture, the expectation that a six-figure salary should be enough to buy your soul! But you have to recognise your own sovereignty in the worst situations and use the power you have within you. My power allowed me to recognise and accept that changing law firms wasn't the answer; the ultimate problem was that I knew I couldn't see myself being a lawyer for the rest of my life. And if I didn't listen to my intuition and exercise my power to do what I did want to do, I'd forever wonder, *What if*? What if I'd followed my dreams and gone after what I wanted? What if I'd focused on what made me happy and lit me up instead of taking the 'sensible' option? What if I'd had the confidence to believe in myself? What could my life have been like? And eventually I decided it was better to try and risk failing than not try and look back with regret.

But that was my choice. I'm not here to tell you to ditch your 9–5 and live life on a beach in Bali. That was the right decision for me (I'm still working on the beach in Bali part). It may not be right for you. To reach the right decision for you, you have to have the confidence to trust yourself to make difficult decisions. Decisions that might seem strange or crazy to everyone else, but feel inherently aligned with who you are now you've got clear on what your values are. You have to use your confidence to push past the resistance and fear to truly believe you can get what you want. And then you have to trust that you can figure out the 'how' along the way.

I know you can do it. And deep down there's a spark inside of you that knows it too. You just need to fan that spark to transform it into a roaring flame.

I want you to feel confident.

Why?

Because confidence is infectious.

The more confident you are, the more confident you make those around you feel. There's a ripple effect that leads to a whole bunch of happy, confident people believing they can do extraordinary things.

I'm rooting for you. And I believe in you. Isn't it time you started believing in yourself?

PART 3
COURAGE

7

CULTIVATING COURAGE

> If you're scared to take chances,
> you'll never have the answers.
>
> – Nas

Now you know what you want (clarity) and you believe you can get it (confidence). The final pillar in this triumvirate is taking action to get after it (courage). The definition of *Courage* is having 'mental or moral strength to venture, persevere, and withstand danger, fear or difficulty'.[10] And it's a necessary step in the journey towards living a life that's Lit!

It's also the hardest step!

See, gaining clarity and boosting confidence is a mindset game. It requires you to sit with your thoughts, delve deep within yourself and rewrite the stories you've

---

10   Merriam-Webster, 'Courage', *Merriam-Webster*, https://www.merriam-webster.com/dictionary/courage, accessed 1 Feb. 2022.

been telling yourself about who you are and what you're capable of. Sure, the process is uncomfortable, but it's a largely solitary act that you can do behind closed doors. No one can see what you're doing.

But taking action, now that's a terrifying prospect. Because no matter how clear you are in your mind about the vision of the life you want and no matter how confident you feel that the vision is possible for you, the thought of verbalising all that, of being seen to be publicly taking steps to achieve all that you want and be all you can be, is absolutely terrifying!

And this is the sad reason why so many people give up on their dreams before they've started and remain stuck living a life of lethargy year after year. They're scared of the unknown. And when you ask them why they're scared, ultimately it comes down to the fact that they're scared of what people might say. I get it! We're wired to care about what people think of us. It's how we evolved as humans. Back in prehistoric times, it was important to be welcomed into your tribe, to have their approval, because if you didn't fit in, if the tribe rejected you, that meant being banished alone into the wilderness to fend for yourself. And that was a dangerous life-threatening prospect.

But I'd like you to stop and think about that for a minute. What are the consequences today of not fitting in with a particular group or of not conforming to a particular way of thinking? Failure? Ridicule? Embarrassment? Have I missed anything? Now ask yourself, are those consequences a price worth paying to live life on your terms? I don't know about you, but in my mind, a bruised ego is definitely a price worth paying to live life Lit!

And as you're reading this book, I'm guessing you've done a quick mental assessment and realised that failure to conform with the popular view won't end up with you being savaged by a wild animal. But not living the life you want will result in an ongoing deterioration of your well-being and a long-term life of lethargy.

That ain't cool! And if you don't want to accept that, you've got to get courageous.

And you should know by now that everything I'm sharing with you in this book is what I've struggled with myself. I've been there, trapped in the mental quicksand, before gaining the knowledge and taking action to pull myself out. That's why I'm so passionate about sharing my experience to help you do the same. I didn't have any special skills, any particular privilege, or any insight into the future. I'm just a guy who decided things had to change and made a decision to do something about it. Which is great news for you as it means there's no reason that you can't do it too!

Speaking of sharing experiences. Here's one of my struggles with courage.

It was March 2020. I'd walked out of BigLaw for the last time at the end of February and I was adjusting to life on the outside (sounds a bit like leaving prison, right?). After eleven years of doing the same thing at the same firm, you'd think it would have taken some time to adjust. But I was on cloud nine! It was as if a huge weight had been lifted off my shoulders, a weight I'd been carrying around for the last five years. And although I was unhappy with how I was treated towards the end (for reasons I won't get into here), as I walked out of that gleaming office building in Singapore's central business district for the final time, I was wearing a smile on my face the size of the Grand Canyon.

I was excited by the possibility of what came next. For the first time in a long time, I felt there was a whole world of opportunity ahead of me. I felt that I could do anything. I'd felt constrained by the BigLaw bubble, trapped on the train, for so long that now it felt like the world was truly my oyster.

But, on the flipside. I had no idea what I was doing. Not. A. Clue.

As I said earlier in this book, I knew I wanted to help people who were in the position I had been in, feeling unfulfilled, unhappy and stuck in a rut. I wanted to help them to see they had a choice and could change their circumstances. I knew the what and my Why, but I had no idea about the how.

What I did know was social media needed to be a part of it. As the extent of the Covid-19 pandemic became more apparent and countries started to close their borders and implement domestic lockdowns, everything was shifting online at a great pace, and I discovered a whole online business world that I never knew existed.

Like most people I knew, I'd had social media accounts for a while. I'd never been a huge social media contributor though. I had a Facebook account that I always toyed with deleting but ultimately kept as I was living overseas and it was the best way to keep in touch with what friends around the world were up to. I had a LinkedIn account that I only used to share the latest law firm deal news we were encouraged to share. And I had an Instagram account that I'd set up on a whim a few years earlier but barely used. I didn't even like contributing to WhatsApp groups as the thought of putting myself out there like that was terrifying. I always felt uncomfortable at large networking or social events. I hated the idea of putting my head above the parapet so publicly and so permanently, fearful of no one engaging or worse, kicking off some social media war. Discovering, through self-reflection, that I was an introvert suddenly made everything make sense.

But I knew that being an introvert didn't mean I could sit in my room and expect people to find me. I had a mission. And to execute that mission and have the impact I wanted to have, people needed to know who I was and how I could help them. So I took an Instagram course (where I realised I knew even less than I thought I did), set up a new Instagram account, and started creating a few posts to share.

And then I procrastinated!

I wrote, read, rewrote, reread, and asked my wife to read each post I'd written as I agonised over the decision to share them.

☑ *What would people say?*

☑ *What if I made a mistake?*

☑ *What if people didn't like what I had to say?*

☑ *What if no one engaged?*

All these questions were swimming around my head.

This procrastination continued for a few weeks. Then, in my own special way of doing things when I commit to something, one day without fanfare I clicked 'post'. And with that, the new me, the former BigLaw lawyer, aka the BigLaw dropout, was officially launched to the world. It was messy, it was ugly but guess what, I didn't die and the world didn't end!

Posting that first post didn't stop me agonising over the next one and the next, but the first step had been taken. I'd taken action. And once I'd got past that first step, the next step didn't seem as scary. Don't get me wrong, the next few posts followed a similar routine of procrastination, but with each post, it got a little bit easier.

And now, sharing my thoughts, my stories, and my vision is the most natural thing in the world. Which is kind of obvious because otherwise you wouldn't be reading this book! But without taking that first step, hitting send on my first post and doing it scared, I never would have written this book.

There's an old saying 'Fortune favours the brave.' It doesn't mean brave people get all the money (although it would be great if it did). It means that those who have the courage to step forward, to step into the arena and take on their biggest fears, will prosper.

But I want to distinguish this type of courage, the courage I'm talking about, from the fairy tales you were told as a child. You know the ones where the brave knight in shining armour (always white and always male) saves the damsel in distress (always blonde and always helpless) by slaying the dragon or some other mythical beast (always dangerous and always 'other'). With the prevalence of these narratives in our childhoods is it any wonder that courage is seen as something that only a select few possess and anyone who pushes back against the status quo is viewed with suspicion.

But unlike the fairy tale narrative, courage needn't be that dramatic. Courage can be found in everyone and in the small actions you take each day. Actions that may make you feel a little uncomfortable but that advance your agenda.

Courage is putting yourself out there and laying yourself bare to criticism or ridicule. It's saying the unpopular thing not because it's unpopular but because you believe in it and it's the right thing to do. It's acknowledging that the situation you're in isn't working for you and not being afraid to take action, burn everything down if you need to, and make changes without any guarantee of success.

So, when you think of courage, don't think of the knight slaying the dragon and beat yourself up for not doing that. Courage can simply mean doing something you haven't done before – something that's a little outside of your zone of comfort.

With each step forward, beyond the familiar, you exercise and strengthen your courage muscle. And by stacking courageous step on top of courageous step, in a process I call courage stacking, what was once scary becomes easy and the next step ahead becomes easier to take.

Like confidence, we all have courage inside of us. It's just that some of us shy away from displaying it for fear of what others might say or what the repercussions might be.

But courage is what will take you from where you are to where you want to be. Courage is what will lead you to that life you've envisioned:

☑ the life where you're not beholden to someone else's agenda

☑ the life where your evenings and weekends are your own

☑ the life where you're treated as a valued member of a team instead of a resource

☑ even the life where you end each day feeling you've made a positive impact on the world.

Each of these things, feelings and emotions lies on the other side of courage. They lie beyond that next courageous step.

So I encourage you to start exercising your courage muscle today. Think of something that seems uncomfortable and commit to doing that thing today. Maybe strike up a conversation with the barista who makes your coffee at the coffee shop, maybe share your opinion on social media about a book you read, maybe write an article about something you're passionate about and post it as a blog, whatever you feel you need to do to move forward towards what you want. And if the thought of any of my suggestions instantly brings you out in a cold sweat and has you hyperventilating, it's OK to dial it back a bit. The idea is not to shake you to your core with fear. The idea is to pick something that's uncomfortable but doable so that you'll keep moving forward and next time you can stack another uncomfortable act on top of the one you previously completed. Hence courage stacking.

Check out the next two chapters for tips on how to build and stack courage. And who knows, maybe you'll be out there casually slaying dragons one day. (Although as a vegan, I'd prefer it if you didn't!).

8

YOU CAN DO HARD THINGS

If you do what is easy, your life will he hard, but if you do what is hard, your life will be easy.

– Les Brown

As humans we're wired to opt for the easiest route to get to where we want to get to. Makes sense, right? I mean we've evolved to be efficient, to conserve energy, to take things easy, because with the familiar we know where we are and our brain can relax knowing that we're safe.

Change disrupts that feeling of safety.

Because change is unfamiliar. Change is hard. Change is scary. Change is uncomfortable. And that's why, even with the best intentions, many people stop pursuing what they want when the time comes to take action. Even when they know that change is necessary to get to where they want to be, they look ahead at all the things they would need to do to overcome the discomfort they would have to endure, and they decide to stay where they are.

Sure, it's the easiest option. But, as the opening quote to this chapter states, easy is only easy in the short term. The only reason you even think about change is because you want to make a situation better. You want to escape a circumstance that isn't working for you, a toxic situation that's draining your energy, affecting your well-being, leaving you living a life of lethargy. So, if you always opt for what's easy, you'll always be where you don't want to be, which, as I said at the start of this book, is going to have a long-term effect on the quality of your health, your relationships, and your life!

Now look, I'm not here to tell you what you should do; it's your life. And, of course, you're entitled to take the easy option and settle for what you have instead of striving for what you want. Sometimes that might be the best option. I'm certainly not saying life should always be hard or that you should live life in a permanent state of discomfort. I mean, I'm all about the Lit! life.

But if you never embrace change, if you never do hard things in life, you'll never move forward. You'll never grow. You'll never get what you truly want.

We're conditioned to fear the unknown. We're sold all the things to make life as comfortable as possible, and we're led to believe that our zone of comfort is the best place to be. We're positively encouraged to reside there.

We have remote controls so we don't have to get up from the TV to change the channel; food delivery services so we never have to cook a meal; the likes of TaskRabbit, Fiverr and Upwork where we can hire people to do the things we don't want to do.

And look, I love creature comforts as much as the next person. Give me some salted popcorn, a glass of champagne, a bingeable Netflix series and a comfortable couch and I'm all set for the night! But the difference is that over time I've reframed my reasoning for embracing these comforts. Before I embraced them to numb the lethargy, to provide an escape from thinking about all the ways my life wasn't how I wanted it to be. Now I see these comforts as integral to my purpose. They save me time and energy and allow me to recharge so that I'm better equipped to pursue my mission.

You see growth doesn't happen in our comfort zone. Growth happens when we get comfortable with being uncomfortable. Growth happens when we try new things, learn new skills and leap into the unknown.

There's a quote from LinkedIn co-founder and venture capitalist Reid Hoffman about entrepreneurship:

'An entrepreneur is someone who will jump off a cliff and assemble an airplane on the way down.'

I think this quote applies not just to entrepreneurship, but to any life arena we step into for the first time. Let me expand on this a little bit.

I talked earlier in this book about my time in the music business and how much to my parent's dismay, I dropped out of university in my second year to follow that path. As I told you earlier I was broke, and the money I was being paid meant I barely had anything left over after paying rent and buying food each month. But I had the courage of my convictions, so I jumped off the cliff! And on the way down, during the four years I spent in the music industry, I grew far more as a person and learned more about life than I ever would have done if I'd stayed at university to complete my degree. Maybe it was because I was getting the opportunity to live my lifelong dream, or maybe it was the exuberance of youth, but I knew within my bones that I could figure things out. I knew that staying at university was unlikely to get me to where I wanted to be so the options were do what I felt I should do, the thing that was easy and expected, or leap off the cliff! I had clarity as to what I wanted and an unshakeable confidence that I could achieve it. Clarity and confidence got me to the edge of the cliff, but it was courage that allowed me to jump!

Courage is what drives you to do those hard things. Courage is what makes you do the thing you want to do, because it lights you up, because it's the right thing to do, all without knowing how it's going to turn out. Without any guarantee of a positive outcome, courage pushes you to do the thing anyway.

But don't get it twisted. Just because you're brave enough to jump, it doesn't mean that everything instantly gets better. You're going to have to deal with some discomfort. And that's hard to deal with, especially when you're used to being a successful high achiever. You have to get comfortable with getting things wrong, with not having a manual for success, with not knowing what you're doing all the time, and with the fact that, in all likelihood, you're going to be terrible the first few times you try something new. Even if you don't think you're terrible at the time, you'll look back one day and cringe.

I see this all the time in my own life. Reading old articles or Instagram captions I've written, or when I was in BigLaw, looking back at a deal I'd worked on years earlier and beating myself up over typos or clunky drafting that had passed me by.

But that's the beauty of being consistent. The more you do something, the better you get at it. You may not become an expert or the best in your field, but you will get better. The catch is you have to have the courage to take that first step and be OK with being shit for a while. In public. In front of real people. Sometimes lots of people! And you have to be OK with seeing the pity in someone's eyes as your latest venture bombs or your social media post gets no engagement. And you have to be OK with knowing that some people are secretly willing you to fail, sniggering behind your back as they say, 'I told you so,' or ask, 'Just who do you think you are?'

That's why you need courage. To keep you moving forward and help you disregard all of this noise. Because you're going to have to put yourself out there if you're going to succeed in getting what you want, in living life Lit!

If you could take your first few steps in secret, without anybody watching, only venturing out into the world once you had a certain level of expertise, would you be more likely to initiate change?

I'm going to guess you answered yes to that question.

But the thing is that change, real change, requires you to take bold action. Not necessarily grandiose action but bold in the sense that the change, and the tools to effect that change, must be visible. We can all sit around theorising, doing work that keeps us busy but doesn't actually take us any closer to achieving our goals. But to move the needle, visible action has to be taken at some point. And once that action is visible, everybody, and I mean everybody, will have an opinion.

Growth is ugly. If people saw you one day as a caterpillar, then the next day as a beautiful butterfly, fully formed and majestic, that would be easy. But a caterpillar has to go through an ugly metamorphosis to become a butterfly, it's not instantaneous. The same applies to you. You will go through pain, discomfort, overwhelm, and fear, to name but a few emotions. You'll make mistakes, and people will see you make those mistakes. That's the hard part, but you can do it, right? I mean, to revisit a question I posed earlier in this book, isn't a bruised ego a price worth paying for living the life you want?

I've been told many times that quitting BigLaw was a courageous thing for me to do. To turn my back on a well-paid career and the status that goes along with it. And while I often dismiss that notion, in writing this book, I guess I can see why people say that. In walking away from an eleven-year career I once again jumped off a cliff. And I'm still building my airplane on the way down.

But what I need you to know is that I don't have some unique superpower that allowed me to do that. I had fears. I have fears. And those fears don't go away. But I did it because it was the right thing for me to do, to, as author Susan Jeffers said, 'feel the fear and do it anyway.'[11] To embrace the unknown and see what's on the other side. Because the way things were wasn't working, and I knew that unless I took proactive steps to change it, I'd still be there, years on, having the same conversations, carrying that same feeling of lethargy and complaining about the same damn things.

I couldn't have gotten to that realisation if I'd continued doing things the same way I'd always done them. It took me doing the inner work and becoming aware of my resistance to change and doing hard things. I had to get really honest with myself, call myself out on my bullshit and work through the years of conditioning that were keeping me stuck. Doing all this helped me see that I could build the courage to get off the train, even if everybody else was continuing the journey.

See, it's those with the courage to advocate for themselves who move forward in life. But I get that fear can be overwhelming sometimes and keep you standing still. So I'd like to share something that helped me look at things differently.

What if, instead of focusing on your fears and discomfort, you focused on the effect that having the courage to change what doesn't serve you, the courage to

---

11   Susan Jeffers, *Feel the Fear and Do It Anyway* (London, 2019).

live life the way you want, would have on the people around you?

Think how they'd feel to have a more focused, motivated, inspiring and happier you!

See, when you're in a good place, living life the way you want to live it, you show up better for those who need you most. Like I said about confidence, there's a ripple effect. Your vibe affects their vibe.

Conversely, when you aren't where you want to be, staying there isn't just bad for you, it's terrible for every relationship you hold dear. You know how you are when you're miserable at your job, you carry that misery back home with you, and it affects your relationship with your partner, your kids, and your friends. Wouldn't life be so much better if you could change that?

So the way I see it you have two choices:

1. Choose fear, stay living in lethargy, and bring down the vibe of everyone around you; or
2. Choose change, be courageous, set yourself free, and bring joy.

Which one will you choose?

As ice hockey legend Wayne Gretzky said, 'You miss 100% of the shots you don't take.'

So this is a call to action to you, dear reader. Start building the courage to take your shot and get after what you want. I can't guarantee that things will work out exactly as you planned, but I can guarantee that if you don't try, you'll never know. And that, my friend, would be a travesty.

THE ART OF
COURAGE STACKING

Courage is what you earn when you've been through the tough times and you discover they aren't so tough after all.

– Malcolm Gladwell

So how do you build this all-important courage? This is where I disappoint you by saying there's no magic courage pill you can buy from your local pharmacy. The only way to build courage is by doing the things you want to build courage for!

You see courage is built by taking action! You can theorise all you want, train your mind to be prepared for all eventualities, but ultimately you have to take action to build your courage muscle.

Treat courage building like working out in the gym. The first few times you go to the gym your technique is poor, you can't lift much and you tire easily. But the more you work out, the stronger you get, the better your technique becomes, and what was once difficult now becomes easy, allowing you to move on to lifting heavier weights that you previously thought were way out of reach for you.

Building courage is the same process. There are levels to this. The more you exercise your courage muscle, the more you do courageous things, and the easier it becomes to take action.

As I said in chapter 7, I call this approach to building courage, *Courage Stacking*. By taking a step outside of your comfort zone each day and challenging yourself to do something that's a little uncomfortable, you continuously build upon the uncomfortable things you've done before. You stack courageous act upon courageous act, allowing you to keep taking action and doing harder things with greater ease and less trepidation.

I know courage stacking works because it's what I've done in my own life to keep levelling up, pushing the boundaries of what I thought I was capable of, and doing hard things.

You know what's coming now, right? An illustrative tale to show you I'll never recommend something that I haven't done myself. Going back to my social media naïveté that I talked about in chapter 7, the way that I evolved and developed my free posting, creative, IDGAF flow was by using courage stacking. The reason I can now post without procrastination and fear is because I envision building the action in front of me on top of the action that previously engendered that same feeling.

After getting comfortable with posting images and captions on my feed, I knew I wanted to start showing up on video. Why? Because although it terrified me, the personal development work I'd done up to that point had got me into that conquer your fears mindset. I also knew that if I wanted people to hear the message I had to share, they needed to feel like they knew me and trusted me. And building trust through generic quote cards is more difficult than showing up raw and unfiltered on camera.

At this point, some of the anxieties about putting myself out there and sharing my thoughts had been removed as I began shedding my BigLaw skin and stepping into my new persona as the BigLaw dropout. I gave myself a pep talk and figured all I needed to do was leverage the courage I'd already built and apply that courage to video. So, as I often do to kick my ass into gear, I set myself a challenge. The challenge was to show up on Instagram Stories every day in September 2020. That's thirty days of turning my iPhone to my face, speaking into it, and sharing it on Instagram for anyone who cared to watch it. I'm not gonna lie, even with all the pep talks and preparation, it was a terrifying prospect. All the old questions of *Who cares? No one's gonna watch, you have nothing to say that anyone wants to hear* and all the negative self-talk you can think of were playing in my head like a negative thought disco. But again, using the gym analogy, I needed to build my courage muscle, so consistency was key.

Now, I don't want you to think that, once you've stacked courage a few times and have the makings of a pretty good-looking courage wall, everything becomes a breeze. You'll still get the butterflies or feel that horrible sinking feeling in the pit of your stomach before doing certain things.

But that's fine. Lean in and embrace that feeling. It means you're challenging yourself. You're growing. You're entering your discomfort zone. And, as I've said before, the discomfort zone is where the magic happens.

Let's get one thing straight though. There's a difference between discomfort and suffering, and I don't want you to suffer. How will you know if you're suffering? Well, I'll put it like this: if what you're about to do renders you with so much fear it literally freezes you, if you genuinely believe you could harm yourself by proceeding and this paralyses you with fear, if your well-being is suffering, e.g. shortness of breath, panic attacks, then you may have crossed the line into suffering.

Or not!

I can't say categorically because we all have a different threshold and tolerance for discomfort. You know when you're in a gym class and the trainer shouts, 'Do as many reps as you can until you can't do anymore!' you know, deep down, whether the reps you did were really the maximum you could do or whether you could have squeezed out a couple more if you'd really wanted to.

So it's down to you and your conscience where the line is between discomfort and suffering. I invite you to push to the edge of the line as often as you can. And each time you do, imagine that line moving a little bit further away, widening your zone of, and tolerance for, discomfort. Because, unlike suffering, discomfort isn't a bad thing. Your brain, in its quest to keep you safe, freaks out at discomfort and, as I said before, society conditions you to seek out comfort in your daily life.

I'm not saying that taking things easy from time to time or chillaxing in comfort is wrong. Who wouldn't want to be comfortable? I'm the guy who loves holidaying in five-star resorts and drinking champagne. I love comfort!

But treating the comfort zone as a destination, instead of a place to check into once in a while to recharge, stunts your growth and ultimately confines you to a life of lethargy. And lethargy is miserable.

So here's my rallying cry to you: step out of that comfort zone, embrace the discomfort and push yourself to get after what lights you up. Life is for living the way you want to live it. There's no point living someone else's dream! Where's the joy in that?

CONCLUSION

DO IT YOUR WAY

During your life, never stop dreaming.
No one can take away your dreams.

– Tupac Shakur

The purpose of this book, and The Triple C Method®, is to get you questioning everything about your life and the way you're living it. Not because you're doing it wrong, but the opposite, to find out if you're doing it the right way for you.

Are you drifting through life in a haze of lethargy, surviving rather than thriving, dreaming wistfully about what your life could be but not taking any steps to make those dreams a reality? Well, I hope this book has sparked something inside you. I hope it's created a burning desire to change all that and become the person you believe you're meant to be. I hope you're now questioning decisions you've made in the past and looking at the choices you make in the present, asking yourself whether you made those decisions and choices because they're what you wanted or what you thought you should want.

An action that helped me look at decisions critically through the lens of whether something was right for me and aligned with my values was writing a purpose statement. A statement about what I wanted to do. Who I wanted to become. What I wanted to be remembered for. Writing that statement was such a powerful exercise and helped me lean even deeper into my mission that it's now something I do with my clients. I haven't shared my statement before, but as you've bought my book and stuck with me to the bitter end, I think you deserve an exclusive, so here it is:

> The purpose of my life is to be generous, supportive, courageous and honest. To spread joy, raise ambition and expand belief in what's possible so that I can help people realise they don't have to do what they've always done and they don't have to be what they've always been.

And that's what I want this book to do for you. I want this book to encourage you to raise your ambition for yourself, your belief in what's possible for you. I want this book to encourage you to question the status quo, and not accept that the way things are is the way they have to be. I want this book to inspire you to take action to get after the life you want. To reframe what you thought was possible and start making moves towards escaping a life of lethargy and living a life that's Lit!

I don't want you to have to go through the wilderness that I did. Sure, I found my purpose in the end, but it took me five years from when I realised that the life I had wasn't the life I wanted to figure it out. That's

Five years of procrastination.

Five years of self-doubt.

Five years of limiting beliefs.

Five years of thinking *Suck it up, next year will be better*.

Five years of living a life of lethargy.

Five years to realise that the life I wanted wasn't going to fall into my lap and change wouldn't happen unless I made it happen. To realise that I had a choice.

And that choice was to take control of my destiny, figure out what I wanted, and get after it; or

Stay in BigLaw, remain unfulfilled, and live with the regret of not attempting to find out what was possible for me.

It took me five years to make the right choice for me. I don't want it to take five years, for you.

See, the best-case scenario is that you stay feeling the same way you do now all the way into next week, next month, next year. And you might be thinking to yourself that although you don't want that, you could tolerate that feeling if it meant you didn't have to embrace the discomfort that inevitably appears when you try hard things.

But here's the thing. If you stay in lethargy, it will eventually bring you down. It will lead to burnout, destruction of your physical and mental well-being, unhappiness, unfulfillment, the list goes on! And I don't want that for you. I don't want that for anyone. And I'm sure you don't want that for yourself. That's why you picked up this book. To find another way.

I want you to live the life you want to live the way you want to live it. I want you to feel empowered to change your situation and break out of your mental cell of self-limitation like I did mine.

But, and this is very important, I don't want you to finish this book thinking you've been doing it all wrong. To think that you need fixing. You don't! Really you don't. No matter what anyone tells you, you don't need fixing. You're not even stuck. You just haven't been here before. You haven't had anyone show you what's possible. You haven't had someone tell you it's OK to do things differently. To think differently. To go left when everyone else is telling you to go right. You haven't had anyone share tools and strategies that moved them from where they were and set them on the path to where they wanted to be, and told you – no, showed you – through their own life stories that you can do it too!

But something made you pick up this book. And rather than leave it gathering dust on the shelf, something also made you read it. So now you know anything is possible for you if you let go of the 'shoulds' and follow your 'wants'. Because by reading this book, you've taken that first step.

It all starts with self-awareness. With knowing yourself intimately. Knowing your hopes, your fears, your values, your mission.

It starts with knowing what lights you up and what dims your shine. It's knowing what your perfect day looks like, down to what you'd do, what you'd wear, how you'd feel. Knowing what's worth fighting for and what you can let go of.

Until I started looking inward and getting to know who I was, what energised me, and what I wanted out of life, I couldn't understand why the money, the status, and the 'success' of being a BigLaw lawyer wasn't making me happy.

But I saved myself from continuing down the lethargy road. I gained that self-awareness and came to know what I wanted my life to be. Somewhere between leaving the music business and working in BigLaw, I lost myself. My values became skewed and unaligned with who I was. I thought I wanted what I had. After years of being broke, I thought the money and status would make me happier. And when I realised they didn't, that they couldn't make up for how I felt, I couldn't see a way out because I didn't know who I would be if I wasn't Ryan Spence, the BigLaw lawyer.

But clarity, confidence and courage helped me change course. They helped guide me back to who I am and start living life the way I wanted to live it.

And that is why the three Cs, The Triple C Method®, underpins the work I do with my clients and the work I continue to do on myself. Because once you know what you want, what you need and where you want to be in life, you begin to look at life through a different lens.

Everything I share in this book is what worked for me and what's worked for my clients. But everyone's different. You may be one of the lucky ones. What you're doing right now may be so right for you that you can't imagine wanting to do anything else. Your life may already be Lit! If this is you, I'm happy for you. Truly I am, because that's what I want for everybody. It's how everyone deserves to live. And, to keep it real, I'm even happier that you took the time to read this book! Now go buy a copy for someone who needs it! (*Joking, not joking.*) Yet even if this is you, I'm sure you have unfulfilled dreams and a niggling feeling that there's something more out there for you, that there's another level of fulfilment, happiness, litness available to you. I hope this book has helped you to tap into that and consider what you can do to achieve that other level.

And if this isn't you ... If you're not where you want to be ... If you're like I was, wandering around directionless in a life of lethargy, I hope this book has opened your mind to the fact that there's a brave new world of opportunity out there for you if you walk to the edge of the cliff and take a leap. And I hope it's made you question what's possible for you and shown you that what's realistic is whatever you make real.

In this book and the accompanying workbook, there are tools and strategies to help move you forward and start taking action towards living the life you want, right now! They don't cover everything, but they do give you what you need to get started. Don't measure success in money, status or things, but in the feeling you get from being in control of your destiny. The feeling you get from working towards something bigger than yourself. If you never try, you'll never know what could have been. The Triple C Method® is the catalyst you need to stop wishing your life was different and start taking action to make it happen, to create the life you want. There's no better time to start your journey to living a Lit! life than now. So stand strong, hold your head high, and get after what you want, my friend. Starting right now! Design and live the life you want. A life that's Lit!

ACKNOWLEDGEMENTS

Support can come in many forms. It can come from someone you know personally who gives a helping hand when you ask for one. It can come from someone you'll never know who speaks your name in a room you're not present in. It can come from someone you pay to help you work through some shit or learn a new skill. It can come in the form of just being a friend, laughing with you, crying with you, and having your back when others try to stab you in it. It can also come from just seeing someone do something you want to do, showing that it's possible and inspiring you to take action to do it too.

All forms of support assisted me in writing this book, and I'm thankful for each and every person, known and unknown, who helped me get to this point.

First, I'd like to thank my wife, Hazel, for supporting me on the path from BigLaw lawyer to BigLaw dropout. I look forward to the day when we walk into a bookstore and see each of our books on the shelf. I love you!

My two boys, Luca and Rafael, for their zest for life and for providing me with a daily reminder to keep connected to my inner child.

To my main man, Kelechi Okereke. The universe knew what it was doing when it led us to cross paths all those years ago. We've come a long way dude and I thank you for your enduring support, even when I was being a dick (I still cringe at the pizza buzzer episode!). I know you've always got my back and I trust you know I'll always have yours.

My bro, Shane. We've come a long way since the Meadows and it's been a privilege to witness your personal development and growth. Thanks for all the free graphic design and marketing input. Love ya little bro.

My mum and dad. Thanks for always being there even when you didn't understand what I was doing or why I was doing it.

To the coaches I've worked with over the years: Samantha Whetstone, Ruby Lin, Michelle Hannon, Jam Gamble, Pia Edberg, and Vivian Wu. Working with each of you expanded my mind, challenged me to think bigger and made me believe I could do far more than I thought possible. Thank you!

To my clients and former clients, thank you for entrusting me as your coach to guide you on your personal growth journeys and for allowing me to play a small role in your transformation stories.

To my ESM crew: Gemma, Amber, Alexandra, and Neerya. Your support has been phenomenal and I appreciate it more than you know. Being in the mastermind sessions with each of you week after week has expanded my mind and made me a better coach. I know each of you are going to do amazing things and transform many lives.

Thank you to podcast hosts Katie Hardy, Lydia Wilmsen, Clarita Escalante, Becky Rodrigues, Lauren Kay, Willow McDonough, Jayne Jaramillo and Mary Mangia, Cheryl Lau, Nicole Colwell, and Melvin Varghese for inviting me to share my story with you and your audience, for your words of encouragement, and for the work you all do in making the world a little bit better through your podcasts.

To every guest who kindly accepted my invitation to appear on my original podcast, *The Yoga Den Podcast*. Prithiv Raaj Elansharan, Sheranne Wong, Sara Riad, Kim Katre, Frieda Levycky, Pedro Luna, Lindsey Athanasiou, Laura Dobberstein, Will Black, Fiona Callanan, Yvette Tee, Gwendolyn Kam, and Aaron Tan, thank you for giving up your time, sharing your stories and for being all-round awesome humans.

And to every person who has engaged with a post on social media, listened to a podcast I've hosted or guested on, or in any way been inspired by and shared the content I put out into the world – thank you! Your continued support leads to more people hearing my story, which in turn leads to more people building the belief that they can transform their life. You are part of that ripple effect whether you know it or not, and I thank you for the part you play in guiding others to live a life that's Lit!

Ryan Spence is a life coach, author, and speaker, helping corporate professionals design a life that's Lit! A first class law graduate of the University of London, Ryan's prestigious eleven-year career in BigLaw involved him in deals that won the Finance Deal of the Year at the 2018 Asia Legal Awards and the 2019 UN Global Impact Award. When Ryan realised that each rung of the corporate ladder he reached was taking him further from where he wanted to be, he took a leap of faith. Driven by his own experience of corporate life, Ryan has become a passionate leader in the business mindset sphere, coaching professionals to find their version of fulfilment, meaning and joy. Having resided in Singapore for seven years, Ryan now lives in Sheffield in the UK with his wife and their two children.

Subscribe to Ryan's email list at www.iamryanspence. com/the-lit-list.

To discuss booking Ryan for media or speaking events, email hey@iamryanspence.com.

www.IAmRyanSpence.com

@iam_ryanspence

linkedin.com/in/i-am-ryan-spence/

@iam_ryanspence

NEXT STEP

You've read the book. You're inspired. You're motivated. You're fired up! So what's your next step?

If you want to accelerate your growth and transformation with personal support along the way, I can help you with that. To discuss hiring me as your coach to help get you from where you are to where you want to be, head to https://www.iamryanspence.com/work-with-me to book a free thirty-minute consultation.

And if you're thinking you'll wait until the time is right, STOP! As the Chinese proverb goes, 'The best time to plant a tree was twenty years ago. The second best time is now.'

NOTES

CPSIA information can be obtained
at www.ICGtesting.com
Printed in the USA
LVHW110424080422
715631LV00003B/75